FACTS NEW ZEALAND

Compiled by

Nicky Chapman

David Bateman

The many tables in this book have been compiled from data from various sources, and these are acknowledged in the sources and further information section at the back of the book.

Comments on content for future editions are welcome. Please write to the address below Attn NZ Facts, or email bateman@bateman.co.nz

First published by David Bateman Ltd,
30 Tarndale Grove, Albany, Auckland, New Zealand

ISBN 1-86953-509-X

Cover design by Shelley Watson/Sublime Design
Book design and typesetting by Julie McDermid/Punaromia
Printed through Colorcraft Ltd

Contents

Introduction 5

Section 1: Natural history

Location (in space and time) 7
Southern stars 10
Geological history 11
Physical features 14
Earthquakes and volcanoes 20
Climate 23
Ozone and ultraviolet light 27
Wildlife and vegetation 28
National parks and reserves 58

Section 2: People

History 63
Government 77
International relations 98
Defence 102
Population 105
Social framework 116
Religions 121
Languages 123
Social welfare 125
Health 130
Education 149
Justice and law 163
Creation and recreation 171
Gaming and betting 192

Section 3: Resources and economy

Resources 195
Income and work 205
Spending 211
Infrastructure 213
Primary production 226
Tourism 240
Manufacturing 243
Science and technology 245
Overseas merchandise trade 248
National finance 250

Information for visitors to New Zealand 252
Sources and further information 254
Index 268

Introduction

Facts New Zealand is for anyone interested in quickly finding information on New Zealand. It is for students of all ages, those working in tourism or with overseas business connections, all visitors to and within New Zealand, and their hosts.

The material in the book was compiled for the general reader. For those who wish to find more detailed information, there are many websites and reference books cited at the end.

The book is divided into three broad categories: Natural History, People, and Resources and Economy (or place, people and product). This overall structure initially envisaged the book moving from the most solid facts to the most fluid, from geographical data to the latest figures on human economic activities.

However, place and people cannot be separated so simply. All aspects of New Zealand interact with each other, and so all the facts keep changing. A heartening example of this interaction is that, while this book was being compiled, 26 kakapo chicks were born from the world's last 64 of these unique flightless parrots. The survival of nearly all of those chicks was due to intense human effort (see www.kakaporecovery.org.nz).

Facts New Zealand is as accurate as we could make it at the time of printing, but do use it as a kind of website on paper, as a starting point from which to learn still more about this ever-changing and fascinating land and its inhabitants.

My thanks go to Jennifer Mair and Tracey Borgfeldt of David Bateman Ltd, who gave me this opportunity to learn so much about my country; to my wonderfully supportive family and friends (most especially to Gael, Anne, Beth, Paul, Ouma, Granmary and Grandpa); and to the many generous people who helped with the book's research.

SECTION 1

Natural History

Location (in space and time)

- New Zealand is in the south-west Pacific, about 1600 km south-east of Australia.
- Its administrative boundaries extend from 33° to 55° south latitude, and from 160° east to 173° west longitude.
- New Zealand Standard Time is 12 hours ahead of Co-ordinated Universal Time (UTC).
- New Zealand Daylight Time (Summer Time):
  - Begins at 2 am on the first Sunday in October.
  - Finishes at 2 am on the third Sunday in March.
  - Is 13 hours ahead of UTC.
- Chatham Islands Time is 45 minutes ahead of that in New Zealand.

New Zealand Summer Time began in 1928.

New Zealand is close to the International Date Line (180° east, with variants), so the Chatham Islands and Gisborne, in the North Island, along with the kingdom of Tonga, are the first to see the new day.

Distance from Wellington (km)

London	18 810	New York	14 400
Johannesburg	11 785	Vancouver	11 725
Los Angeles	10 790	Beijing	10 750
Santiago	9 370	Tokyo	9 240
Singapore	8 525	South Pole	5 340

New Zealand in the South Pacific

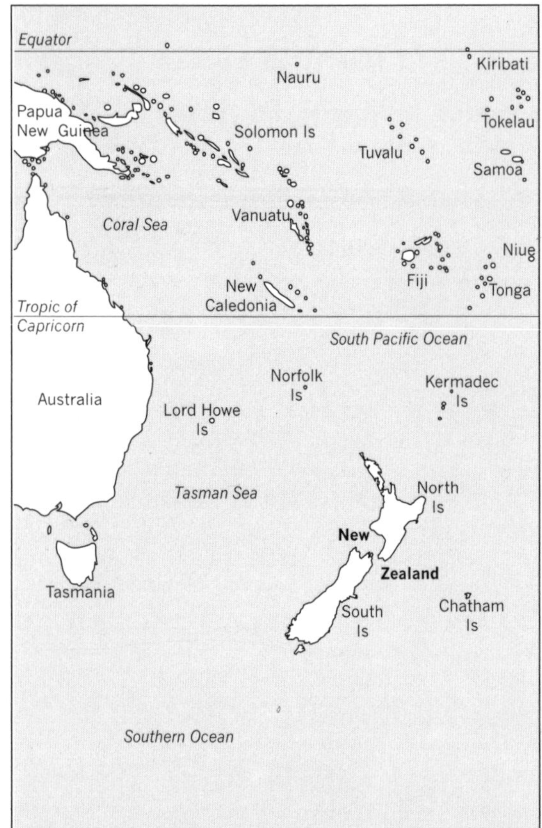

New Zealand: main cities

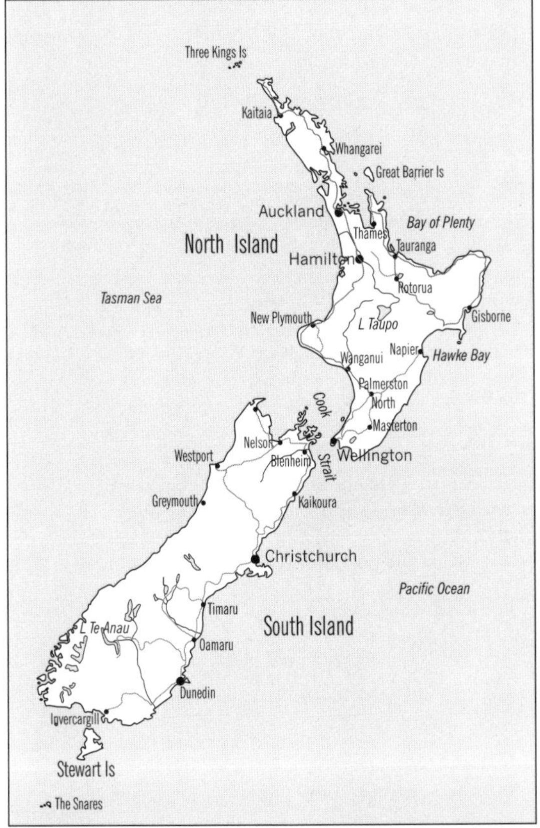

Southern stars

The southern hemisphere constellations, unlike the northern hemisphere ones, are named after animals that the European explorers discovered in their travels and the instruments they used to help navigate their way.

Some southern constellations can never be seen in the north. One such constellation is the Southern Cross, or Crux, and the associated Pointers. These stars can be seen year round from New Zealand.

The true South Pole can be found by using the Southern Cross. Imagine two lines, one extending from the long axis of the cross, and the other at right angles to the Pointers. Below the intersection point is due south.

In mid-winter (June) the Southern Cross appears high in the sky at 8 pm. It is lower in the sky at 8 pm in mid-summer (December), and because the earth has revolved through 180° during the intervening six months it now appears upside down.

An easily seen winter constellation is Scorpius, which passes almost overhead during the evening. In summer, Orion is prominent in the evening sky, but 'stands on his head' from New Zealand.

- Names for constellations are given to the shapes and patterns they create, and most European names for constellations were given to those in the northern hemisphere. However, the patterns they form appear upside down to viewers in the southern hemisphere.
- The Southern Cross is one of the brightest constellations in the southern sky.
- The traditional Maori year with its seasonal activities was determined by the time of rising of the stars.

Geological history

New Zealand is a relatively new landmass, which developed as part of the edge of both Australia and Antarctica when these two continents were part of the Gondwana supercontinent. The country's geological history is a process of sedimentation and uplift, submerging under the sea and rising again, and being forced apart from Gondwana by tectonic plate movement processes, between 120 and 60 million years ago.

New Zealand now lies on the boundary between the Australian Plate in the north-west and the Pacific Plate in the south-east. New Zealand and the continental shelf that surrounds it sit astride the two plates. The deforming plate boundary zone crosses the country diagonally from the north-east to the south-west. The collision of the plates has created a subduction trench in the north-east and another in the south-west. Between them, collision and sliding dominate the South Island, and areas in the western North Island and Cook Strait region are being submerged.

The plate movements mean New Zealand is being compressed but also sheared sideways. This movement results in faulting (and associated earthquakes), deformation and squashing to push up mountains, and volcanic activity.

- Curio Bay in Southland has one of the world's least disturbed examples of a Jurassic fossil forest.
- The best preserved remnant of the Late Cretaceous Peneplain is around Poolburn, Central Otago.
- When New Zealand moved away from Gondwana, it became the most isolated landmass of its size. Carried with it was a selection of plants and animals that evolved in isolation, and which helped give New Zealand some of its unique flora and fauna, such as the moa, tuatara and weta.

Period	Epoch	Millions of years before present (Ma)	Life Forms	Geological Events
Quaternary	Holocene		During the last 'glacial' the windy, dry, cold climate restricted trees to the North Island.	The last 2 million years (the 'Ice Age') have seen about 30 fluctuations between cold and warm periods. In the last cold 'glacial' 20,000 years ago, sea level receded 120 m below present level; NZ was 50% larger than now.
	Pleistocene	2		50–150,000 years ago Auckland volcanism commenced.
Tertiary	Pliocene	5		5 Ma outline of modern NZ taking place with two main islands.
	Miocene	25	Dominant species angiosperm* plants, mammals, birds.	22 Ma volcanic activity and mountain building along Southern Alps begins, uplift continues along Alpine Fault where Pacific and Australian plates meet.
	Oligocene	36		
	Eocene	54		40 Ma most of Rangitata landmass under water.
	Paleocene	65	65 Ma dinosaurs die out.	60 Ma Tasman Sea at full width. 70 Ma Rangitata landmass eroded to a flat low-lying landscape.

Cretaceous		135	80 Ma main plants ferns and conifers (gymnosperms*), flowering plants beginning to evolve. Fauna were tuatara (unchanged to present), dinosaurs, weta ancestors, kiwi and moa ancestors, frogs.	80 Ma Rangitata landmass broke away from Gondwana, at the same time as Australia and Antarctica.
Jurassic		200 230		180 Ma the supercontinent of Pangaea begins to break up. The southern portion, Gondwana, is made up of what will become Africa, South America, India, Australia, Antarctica and the Rangitata landmass (the New Zealand continental crust).
Triassic		300	Reptiles Ferns Araucarian** plants	
Permian				

*Angiosperms are seed-bearing plants, in which the ovules are enclosed in an ovary, which develops into fruit after fertilisation; gymnosperms are plants that reproduce using cones or cone-like structures. They evolved before angiosperms, which reproduce using flowers.

**Araucarian plants are ancient conifers. Modern descendants in the genus include kauri, monkey puzzle and Norfolk Island pine.

Physical features

New Zealand consists of two large islands: North and South (Te Ika a Maui and Te Wai Pounamu), and several smaller ones, of which Stewart Island (Rakiura) and the Chatham and Pitt Islands (Rekohu/Wharekauri and Rangiauria) are the largest inhabited ones. New Zealand also has jurisdiction over the territories of Tokelau and the Ross Dependency. (Island territories administered by New Zealand at various times included the Cook Islands, Western Samoa, Niue and the Tokelaus. The Cooks, Western Samoa and Niue have all gained their independence but still have special associations with New Zealand.)

- New Zealand occupies approximately 27.1 million ha or nearly 270,000 sq km.
- It is predominantly mountainous and hilly country:
  - Over two-thirds (18.5 million ha) slopes at greater than 12° and nearly half at greater than 28°.
  - Approximately three-fifths of the country (16 million ha) is over 300 m above sea level, with one-fifth over 900 m.

Size of main and outlying islands (sq km)

North Island	113 729
South Island	150 437
Offshore islands (over 20 km)	1 065
Stewart Island	1 680
Chatham Islands	963
Raoul Island	34
Campbell Island	113
Total landmass	**268 021**

Note: This total landmass excludes offshore islands under 20 sq km.

Ten largest offshore islands (sq km, rounded)

Great Barrier Island (Aotea Island)	278
Resolution Island	208
Rangitoto ke te tonga (D'Urville Island)	167
Waiheke Island	93
Secretary Island	80
Arapawa Island	76
Matakana Island	60
Little Barrier Island (Hauturu Island)	31
Inch Clutha (near Balclutha)	28
Rangitoto Island	23

Note: Outlying islands are those far from the three main islands. Offshore islands are those close to the main islands of New Zealand.

Ten highest mountains (all South Island) (m)

Aoraki/Cook	3 754
Tasman	3 497
Dampier	3 440
Silberhorn	3 300
Hicks (St David's Dome)	3 198
Lendenfeldt	3 194
Torres	3 163
Teichelmann	3 160
Sefton	3 157
Malte Brun	3 155

The Southern Alps have at least 223 named peaks higher than 2300 m.

Major North Island mountains (m)

Ruapehu	2 797
Taranaki/Egmont	2 518
Ngauruhoe	2 287
Tongariro	1 967

Aoraki/Mt Cook's height was reduced by 10 m on 14 December 1991, when rock slipped from its summit.

Glaciers

There are 3144 glaciers in New Zealand of over 1 ha in area, covering a total area of 1158 sq km. The estimated ice volume is 53.3 cu km.

Five largest glaciers (ha)

Tasman	9 834
Murchison	3 658
Fox	3 469
Franz Josef	3 260
Volta, Therma	2 638

- Nearly 50% of all of New Zealand's ice is contained in the five largest glaciers.
- Glaciers creep downhill at 2.5 cm to 30 m a day. The Franz Josef Glacier averages 1 m a day.

Glaciers and climate change

Glaciers change because of winter snow accumulation or loss, and summer melt losses. They do signal climate change, but not immediately. Some change within years; the larger can take decades. Some glaciers are now receding, while others are advancing.

Ten largest lakes (sq km and maximum depth in m)

Taupo	606	163
Te Anau	344	417
Wakatipu	293	380
Wanaka	193	311
Ellesmere	181	2
Pukaki	169	70
Manapouri	142	444
Hawea	141	384
Tekapo	88	120
Rotorua (10th equal)	80	45
Wairarapa (10th equal)	80	3

Notes: Volcanic lakes are only in the North Island. South Island lakes have mainly been formed by glaciers.
30 South Island lakes are man-made, for irrigation, water supply or hydro-electricity generation.

Ten longest rivers (km)

Waikato	425
Clutha	322
Whanganui	290
Taieri	288
Rangitikei	241
Mataura	240
Waiau	217
Clarence	209
Waitaki	209
Oreti	203

Caves

Ten deepest caves (m)

Nettlebed Cave, Mt Arthur (NW Nelson)	889
Ellis Basin system, Mt Arthur	775
Bulmer Cavern, Mt Owen	749
HH Cave, Mt Arthur	721
Bohemia Cave, Mt Owen	713
Incognito/Falcon, Mt Arthur	540
Viceroy Shaft, Mt Owen	440
Twin Traverse, Mt Arthur	400
Legless, Takaka Hill	400
Greenlink-Middle Earth, Takaka Hill	394

Ten longest caves (m)

Bulmer Cavern, Mt Owen	50 125
Ellis Basin Cave system, Mt Arthur	28 730
Nettlebed Cave, Mt Arthur	24 252
Megamania, Buller	14 800
Honeycomb Hill Cave, Oparara	13 712
Gardner's Gut, Waitomo	12 197
Bohemia Cave, Mt Owen	9 300
Mangawhitikau system, Waitomo	8 054
The Metro/Te Ananui, Buller	8 000
Aurora-Te Ana-au, Te Anau	6 400

There are three main types of caves: those formed in cliffs by the pounding of waves; those in lava flows where the solidified outer crust is left after the molten core has drained away; and those formed in soluble rocks like limestone by water (the most common type in New Zealand). Limestone is brittle and cracks with movement. Rainwater percolates through the surface soil, enters the cracks and dissolves the limestone.

The most notable limestone caves are the Te Kuiti group in the area south of Hamilton (from Port Waikato south to Mokau and inland to the Waipa valley), especially those in the Waitomo district, and the Mount Arthur region in the mountains of north-west Nelson.

The most spectacular features of limestone caves are stalactities, which are formed by solidifying calcium carbonate in water dripping from above, and stalagmites, which build up from the cave floor. They form strange and beautiful shapes in varying colours.

The best-known inhabitants of caves are glow worms and cave wetas. The bones of many extinct birds, including various moa species, have been found in caves, most abundantly in South Island caves.

Geographical extremes

Highest point	Aoraki/Mt Cook, 3 754 m above sea level
Lowest point	Bottom of Lake Hauroko, 306 m below sea level
Largest lake	Lake Taupo, 606 sq km
Deepest lake	Lake Hauroko, 462 m
River with greatest flow	Clutha River, 650 cu m/second
Largest glacier	Tasman Glacier, 28.5 km long
Deepest cave	Nettlebed, Mt Arthur, 889 m deep
Town furthest from sea	Cromwell (approximately 120 km)
Greatest width	450 km
Length of country	>1 600 km

Earthquakes and volcanoes

New Zealand is in the part of the world known as the 'ring of fire', where the Pacific and the Australian plates of the earth's crust meet.

Earthquakes are common in New Zealand, but usually moderate. A shock of Richter magnitude 6 or above occurs about once a year; a shock of magnitude 7 or above once in 10 years; and a shock of about magnitude 8 perhaps once a century.

Earthquake fatalities since 1840 (with Richter scale magnitude)

8 July 1843	Wanganui	7.5	2
16 October 1848	NE Marlborough	7.1	3
23 January 1855	SW Wairarapa	8.2	5
16 March 1901	Cheviot	7.0	1
7 October 1914	East Cape	7–7.5	1
16 June 1929	Murchison	7.8	17
3 February 1931	Hawke's Bay	7.9	256
5 March 1934	Pahiatua	7.6	1
24 May 1968	Inangahua	7.0	3
Total deaths since 1840			**289**

Note: Richter scale

0 to 4.3	Mild
4.4 to 4.8	Moderate
4.9 to 6.2	Intermediate
6.3 to 7.3	Severe
7.4 to 8.9	Catastrophic

Wairarapa earthquake 1855

- At Turakirae Head, the southern end of the Rimutaka Range rose by over 6 m.

- The land shifted about 12 m horizontally along the western edge of the Wairarapa.
- There was one casualty in Wellington, and at least four others in the Wairarapa and Manawatu.
- The earthquake also created a tsunami in Cook Strait and Wellington harbour.

It has been estimated that there is an 8 to 11% probability of a 7.5 Richter scale earthquake occurring along the Wellington fault line within the next 50 years.

Volcanoes

Most New Zealand volcanism in the last 1.6 million years has occurred in the Taupo Volcanic Zone, which extends from White Island to Ruapehu.

The Taupo Volcanic Zone is extremely active on a world scale. It includes three frequently active cone volcanoes (Ruapehu, Tongariro/Ngauruhoe, White Island), and two of the most productive calderas in the world (Okataina and Taupo).

There are three main types of volcano in New Zealand:

- Volcanic fields, such as Auckland, where each eruption builds a single small volcano (e.g. Mt Eden). The next eruption occurs in a different spot in the field.
- Cone volcanoes, such as Egmont/Taranaki and Ruapehu, where a succession of small to moderate eruptions come from one location. These eruptions over thousands of years build the cones.
- Caldera volcanoes such as Taupo and Okataina (which includes Tarawera). These have a history of infrequent but moderate-large eruptions. The caldera-forming eruptions create super craters 10–25 km in diameter and deposit cubic kilometres of ash and pumice.

Deaths in volcanic areas over 150 years

1846	Waihi (Lake Taupo)	Debris avalanche/mudflow from thermal area	c 60
1886	Tarawera Rift	Large volcanic eruption	108–153
1903	Waimangu (Tarawera)	Hydrothermal explosion	4
1910	Waihi (Lake Taupo)	Debris avalanche/ mudflow from thermal area	1
1914	White Island	Debris avalanche from crater wall	11
1917	Waimangu (Tarawera)	Hydrothermal explosion	2
1953	Tangiwai (Ruapehu)	Lahar and flood from crater lake	151
Total deaths since 1846			**>337**

- The most violent eruption on earth in the last 5000 years occurred at Taupo in AD 230. An earlier eruption, 26,500 years ago, was one of the largest ever to occur on earth, ejecting over 800 cu km of material and covering the entire country in at least 1 cm of ash. Lake Taupo (606 sq km) fills the massive caldera.
- Frying Pan Lake near Rotorua is the world's largest hot water spring. It has a surface area of 38,000 sq m, and at its deepest point the water temperature reaches 200°C. The hot springs, geysers and mudpools around Rotorua are part of a volcanic system.
- Ruapehu, Ngauruhoe and White Island are among the most frequently active volcanoes in the world. Ruapehu has been active since September 1995 and White Island is constantly steaming.
- Auckland is built on and among 48 volcanoes that have erupted over the last 140,000 years. The youngest, at just 600 years old, is Rangitoto.

Climate

New Zealand is a long, narrow, mountainous country, surrounded by ocean. Its climate is mainly influenced by:

- Its location in the Southern Temperate Zone, in a latitude range with prevailing westerly wind flow.
- Its oceanic environment. Most of New Zealand has an 'island' climate, apart from the alpine areas and Central Otago. Central Otago is more like a continental area, with dry, hot summers and cold winters.
- Its mountains. The main mountain ranges deflect weather systems, coming mostly from the west, bringing rain to upland and upwind areas and drier conditions downwind. New Zealand's complex landscape is reflected in its climate patterns, which make weather forecasting a demanding task.

Cook Strait, between the North and South Islands, is the main gap between the mountain ranges of each island. It acts as a funnel for air flow onto the country and so is a particularly windy area. Foveaux Strait, between the South and Stewart Islands, acts in much the same way.

January and February are New Zealand's warmest months and July is normally the coldest.

The climate is temperate (averages range from 8°C in July to 17°C in January), but summer temperatures occasionally reach the 30s in many inland and eastern regions. Frosty winter nights are common inland in the central North Island and throughout the South Island.

The mean annual rainfall varies widely, from less than 400 mm in Central Otago to over 12,000 mm in the Southern Alps.

For most of the North Island and the northern South

Island the driest season is summer. However, for the West Coast of the South Island and much of inland Canterbury, Otago and Southland, winter has less rainfall.

Humidity is generally between 70% and 80% in coastal areas, and about 10% lower inland. Very low humidities of less than 25% are often reached in the lee of the Southern Alps, particularly with winds like the hot dry 'Canterbury Nor'wester'.

Mean climate measures in four main cities, 1971–2000

	Mean daily max. temperature (°C) Jan	July	Mean annual bright sunshine (hours)	Mean annual rainfall (mm)
Auckland	23.3	14.5	2 024	1 240
Wellington	20.3	11.4	2 065	1 249
Christchurch	22.5	11.3	2 100	630
Dunedin	18.9	9.8	1 585	812

Annual rainfall figures are most variable for parts of North Otago, Canterbury, Marlborough, Hawke's Bay, Gisborne, the Coromandel and Northland. These areas are therefore the ones most susceptible to particularly dry or wet years.

Summary of recorded climate extremes (31 May 2001)

Rainfall (mm)

Highest:

10 mins	34	Tauranga (Bay of Plenty)	17 April 1948
1 hr	109	Leigh (Northland)	30 May 2001
24 hrs	682	Colliers Creek (West Coast)	21–22 Jan 1994
365 days	18 442	Cropp River (West Coast)	29 Oct 1997–29 Oct 1998

Lowest:			
3 mths	9	Cape Campbell (Marl)	Jan–Mar 2001
12 mths	167	Alexandra (Ctrl Otago)	Nov 1963–Oct 1964

Air temperature (°C)

Highest:			
Nth Island	39.2	Ruatoria (East Coast)	7 Feb 1973
Sth Island	42.4	Rangiora & Jordan (Marl)	Feb 1973
Lowest:			
Nth Island	–13.6	Chateau Tongariro	7 July 1937
Sth Island	–21.6	Ophir (Ctrl Otago)	3 July 1995

Sunshine hours (annual)

Highest:			
Nth Island	2 588	Napier (Hawke's Bay)	1994
Sth Island	2 711	Nelson (Marl)	1931

Wind gusts (km/h)

Nth Island	248	Hawkins Hill (Wellington)	6 Nov 1959 & 4 Jul 1962
Sth Island	250	Mt John (Canterbury)	18 April 1970

Snow

- The North Island has a small permanent snow field above 2400 m altitude on the central plateau. In winter snow may fall on any of the mountain ranges, but it rarely settles below 500 m.
- The permanent snow line on the Southern Alps is around 2100 m, with glaciers down as low as 700 m on the eastern flank and 400 m on the steeper western side.

- Snowfall on the Alps can occur in all seasons. In winter it often extends to inland Canterbury and Otago, and occasionally to the coast, but rarely does the winter snow line remain below 1000 m for more than a month.
- Snow sports are popular, and support a major tourism industry.

El Niño and La Niña

El Niño is a natural feature of the global climate system. Originally it referred to the periodic development of unusually warm ocean waters along the tropical South American coast, but now it is more generally used to describe the whole 'El Niño-Southern Oscillation (ENSO) phenomenon'. It is one extreme of the main multi-year cycle in global climate; the other extreme is called 'La Niña'.

El Niño effects upon New Zealand

- Summer: Tendency for stronger or more frequent winds from the west. Consequent drought in east coast areas and more rain in the west.
- Winter: Winds more from the south, bringing colder conditions to the land and surrounding ocean.
- Spring and autumn: South-westerlies stronger or more frequent, providing a mix of the summer and winter effects.

La Niña effects upon New Zealand

- Have weaker impacts on New Zealand's climate.
- Tendency to more north-easterly winds.
- Consequently more moist, rainy conditions to the north-eastern parts of the North Island.

Although El Niño is an important influence on New Zealand's climate, it accounts for less than 25% of the year-to-year variance in seasonal rainfall and temperature at most New Zealand measurement sites.

Ozone and ultraviolet light

Ozone, an atmospheric gas that screens out most of the sun's harmful ultraviolet (UV) rays, has been decreasing worldwide. The average decrease in summertime ozone in the New Zealand region has been about 5% per decade in the last 20 years.

The 'ozone hole' over Antarctica during spring and summer does not reach New Zealand.

UV levels over New Zealand are highest in summer, from 12 to 2 pm, under cloudless skies, and in the north of the country.

In recent years, the break-up of the Antarctic ozone hole has occurred later, in mid-summer, and has further increased UV levels over New Zealand. This is because ozone-poor air from above the Antarctic mixes with the air above New Zealand at the same time that the sun is high in the sky. There is thus less ozone protection from UV light at the time of year when UV levels are at their highest due to the sun's position.

Wildlife and vegetation

New Zealand separated from the Gondwana supercontinent about 80 million years ago. Some of the original inhabitants endured while other species died out. Before human contact, New Zealand plants and animals were unusual because of the absence of snakes, land mammals (apart from three species of bat) and many of the flowering plant families. Another unusual feature was the evolution of many large and flightless birds and insects. The world's tallest bird was the extinct giant moa.

New Zealand's land-based plants and animals evolved in the absence of mammalian plant browsers or predators, which makes them extremely vulnerable to introduced predators (such as rats and cats) and competitors (such as deer and possums).

Around 90% of New Zealand's insects and marine molluscs, 80% of trees, ferns and flowering plants, 25% of bird species, all 60 reptiles, four remaining frogs and two species of bat are found nowhere else on earth.

Humans introduced many new species (since 1840 over 80 species of mammal, bird and fish and more than 1800 plant species), totally changing the landscape and ecology.

New Zealand has very few poisonous or dangerous land animals. There are no snakes, and the rare katipo spider is the only native venomous creature.

Whole orders and families are found only in New Zealand: tuatara, moa and kiwi, all of the native lizards, and all the native earthworms (178 species) to name just a few. Moa are extinct, but other large flightless birds remain. Flightless insects are numerous including many large beetles and 70 or so endemic species of the cricket-like weta.

New Zealand has 87 species of seabirds. About 400 different marine fish are resident in the waters around New Zealand as well as various species of seal, dolphins and porpoises.

Thirty-two species of whale have been recorded and three of the largest (sperm, humpback and right) regularly migrate here in spring and autumn.

Most endangered taxa

The World Conservation Union (IUCN) periodically publishes 'Red Lists' of globally threatened taxa (that is, categories of living things, such as the different species of plants and animals). This Red List system has seven threatened categories, ranging from Extinct to Least Concern.

New Zealand's Department of Conservation (DOC) follows a similar system, but it has been adapted for New Zealand conditions. These categories provide an indication of the level of threat of extinction that taxa face. They are:

Acutely Threatened:

1. Nationally Critical
2. Nationally Endangered
3. Nationally Vulnerable

Chronically Threatened:

4. Serious Decline
5. Gradual Decline

At Risk:

6. Sparse
7. Range Restricted

An example of how these levels of risk are assessed (based on population sizes and predicted rate of decline) is given in the following definition of the 'Nationally Critical' level: 'A taxon is Nationally Critical when available scientific evidence indicates that it meets any of the following three criteria:

1. The total population size is <250 mature individuals.
2. Human influences have resulted in <2 sub-populations *and either:*
   a. <200 mature individuals in the largest sub-population, *or*

b. the total area of occupancy is <1 ha (0.01 sq km).

3. There is a predicted decline of >80% in the total population in the next 10 years due to existing threats.' (See Molloy et al., in the bibliography.)

Origins of New Zealand plants and animals

Examples of Gondwana origins

Kauri (conifers)
Kahikatea (podocarps)
Tuatara
Frogs
Large carnivorous snails
The ratite ancestors of the kiwi and moa

Examples of tropical origins

Nikau palm and tree ferns
Tropical snails
Some earthworms

Examples of Australian origins

Manuka
Parakeets
Tui
Many wetland birds

Examples of Pacific origins

Pohutukawa
Many ferns
Migratory birds like the shining cuckoo

Examples of subantarctic or circumpolar origins

Beeches
Penguins, albatrosses, petrels
Fuchsias

Examples of cosmopolitan mountain elements

(Entered via mountain and island chain from South-east Asia.)
Buttercups, daisies, veronicas, gentians

Of recent human introduction

Very many species of animals and plants: see lists following.

Selected groups of introduced and native species

Group	Introduced species	Native species	Percentage endemic
Marine algae	3*	900*	43%
Bryophytes:			
– mosses	8	516	21%
– liverworts	5*	525*	–
Ferns and allies	26	189	46%
Conifers	28	20	100%
Flowering plants	1 842*	1 813	84%
Earthworms	40	178	100%
Land snails/slugs	12	520*	99%
Spiders/harvestmen	60	2 500*	90%
Insects	1 100	9 460*	90%
Freshwater fish	23*	27	85%
Amphibians	3	7*	100%
Reptiles:			
– land	3	62*	98%
– marine	–	6	–
Birds:			
– land/freshwater	41	84	54%
– marine	0	87	20%
Mammals:			
– land	33	3	100%
– marine	1	34	6%

* Estimated.

Worst New Zealand pests

Mammals	Date of introduction
Rat	1769 (debated)
Pig	1773
Goat	1773
Cat	c. 1800
Mouse	1824
Rabbit	1777
Possum	1858
Deer	c. 1851–60 (debated)
Ferret	c. 1867–69 (debated)
Wallaby	1870
Stoat/weasel	1885
Thar	1904
Chamois	1907
Insects	
Housefly	c. 1830
Codlin moth	c. 1870
Tomato caterpillar	1907
Cabbage butterfly	1929
German wasp	1944
Plants	**Date first noted as noxious**
Blackberry	1838
Thistle	1859
Gorse (north of Canterbury)	1859
Horned poppy	1870s
Ragwort	1874
Paspallum	1895
Willow	1950

Forests

Most (78%) of New Zealand was forested just before human arrival. One-third of the forests were cleared by pre-European Maori, and a further third has been cleared over the last 160 years. Now only 23% of New Zealand is forested, much in mountainous areas, and most of this is protected.

Native forest and light woodland cover in different periods (millions of hectares, approx.)

Pre-Polynesian	21.1
Early European (1840)	14.0
Present	6.2

Types of New Zealand forest

New Zealand has two main types of forest:

1. Conifer-hardwoods, dominated by gymnosperms,* mainly podocarps** but also kauri and sometimes cedar.
2. Beech forests, dominated by one or more of the four indigenous beech species.

* Gymnosperms are plants which reproduce using cones or cone-like structures. They evolved before flowering plants (angiosperms).
** Podocarps are generally tall trees, members of an ancient plant family originating from Gondwana.

Conifer-hardwoods

- Are very dense, luxuriant, especially if no browsing introduced mammals are present.
- Have understoreys of small trees, shrubs, ferns, mosses, lichen and many lianes (climbers) and epiphytes.
- Are generally divided into three subtypes:
    1. The kauri-podocarp-hardwood forests which covered most of the northern North Island.
    2. The podocarp-hardwood forests that make up the

lowland rain forests of the North Island and the West Coast of the South Island.

3. The podocarp-hardwood-beech forest found along the mountain ranges of both islands, especially the South Island, below about 650–700 m.

Pure beech forests (montane forests)

- Are more open forests.
- Have fewer understorey species present.
- Are characteristic of the central and southern North and South Islands, above 300 m altitude.
- The bush-line, usually of mountain or silver beech, is usually between 1350 and 1500 m.

Other types of forests

- Coastal trees, such as mangroves, nikau, karaka, pohutukawa.
- Swamp forest, dominated by the podocarp kahikatea, was once extensive, and now prominent in western South Island.
- Secondary forests, including kanuka, manuka and a range of broad-leaved trees and tree-ferns, have developed on abandoned farmland and milled-over older forests in lowland and hilly areas.

- Pure mangrove forests are common in the estuaries of North Auckland.
- At least one out of every 10 New Zealand plants is under threat of extinction in the wild. For example, 180 vascular plant species and subspecies are listed in the three 'Acutely Threatened' categories.

Some plant facts

- The largest kauri on record grew at Mill Creek, Mercury Bay. Measured around 1850, its height was 21.8 m to the first branch, and its girth was 23.43 m. Tane Mahuta, in the Waipoua forest, has a girth of 14 m, is 51 m tall, and is 1200 years old.
- A 28 m tall, 700-year-old kahikatea growing in south Westland may hold the world record for hosting climbing and perching plants. It carries 28 species: seven shrubs, five climbers, 10 ferns, five orchids, and a nest epiphyte. It also has 18 lichens, five mosses and six liverworts.
- Ongaonga the 'fierce' native nettle has killed dogs, horses and at least one human, due to reactions to the 'sting'. The plant is also the host for the red admiral butterfly, whose caterpillars safely feed on it.
- *Hebe* is the largest genus of New Zealand plants, with about 100 species. Many hybrids and varieties of *Hebe* are popular with gardeners around the world.
- About 10% of New Zealand's native shrubs and trees are divaricate, a rare form in all other countries. These plants have small, widely spaced leaves on wiry, interlaced branches. Some divaricate plants like lowland ribbonwood and kowhai change form as they mature, starting life with tough, shrubby divaricate growth, and then swapping to straighter branches and bigger leaves from about 2.5 m.

Recently researchers have used emus and ostriches to show that New Zealand divaricate plants adapted to protect themselves from browsing moa, not just to extreme of climates as previously thought.

Birds

Flightless birds (not extinct)

New Zealand is renowned for its large number of flightless birds. This number is large because the country lacked predatory mammals until the arrival of humans about 1000 years ago. Flightless birds include:

Kakapo (can glide downwards)
Takahe
Weka
Blue penguin (five subspecies)
Erect crested penguin
Fiordland crested penguin
Gentoo penguin
King penguin
Rockhopper penguin
Royal penguin
Snares Island crested penguin
Yellow-eyed penguin
Great spotted kiwi
Little spotted kiwi
South, North and Stewart Island brown kiwi (three subspecies)
Auckland Island teal (subspecies brown teal)
Campbell Island teal (subspecies brown teal)

- The kiwi is the only bird with nostrils at the end of its bill.
- Some migratory birds, such as the eastern bar-tailed godwit and great knot, fly from Siberia and Alaska to New Zealand (a distance of up to 11,000 km) twice a year. It is thought that the bar-tailed godwit prepares by feeding until up to 55% of its body weight is fat.

- The Royal Forest and Bird Protection Society of New Zealand Incorporated (Forest and Bird) is the country's senior conservation organisation. Its aim is to preserve and protect the native plants, animals and natural features of New Zealand. It was founded in 1923, and has over 40,000 members in branches throughout the country.

Summary of bird extremes

World's tallest bird	giant moa (extinct), at probably 3 m.
World's largest bird of prey	New Zealand/Haast eagle (extinct), with 75 mm talons.
Largest moa egg	giant moa, weighing 4 kg.
Most recent bird extinction	bush wren, in 1960s, killed by rats on Big South Cape Island, near Stewart Island.
Rarest bird	fairy tern, with only 36 remaining. Fairy terns (New Zealand's are a subspecies) also breed in Australia.
World's rarest seabird	Chatham Island taiko total population 100–140 birds; only six known nesting burrows.

The kakapo is the world's heaviest and only flightless parrot, with the greatest weight difference between the sexes.

Some places to watch birds

- Australasian gannet colony, Muriwai Beach (an hour's drive north-west of Auckland).
- Tiritiri Matangi Island is home to some rare species of birds that can only be seen in sanctuaries or on islands, and an abundance of more common native species. It can be reached by boat from Auckland or Whangaparaoa Peninsula.

- The Miranda coast in the Firth of Thames is one of the most important shorebird areas in the country, especially for viewing a wide variety of wading species.
- Ahuriri Wetlands, Napier. This estuary supports a large and varied population of birds on tidal mudflats and coastal waters.
- Mt Bruce National Wildlife Centre, Wairarapa, a breeding centre for rare native birds.
- Kapiti Island is a closed sanctuary and is home to many rare birds. Visitors are limited to 50 per day and bookings must be made well in advance (contact the Kapiti Booking Line, Department of Conservation, at the Wellington Conservancy).
- The Manawatu Estuary is perhaps best known for the wide variety of Arctic-breeding migrant wading birds that occur here over the summer.
- Okarito White Heron colony at the Okarito Lagoon, South Westland.
- Royal Albatross Centre, Otago Peninsula, Dunedin, is the only mainland breeding colony for the royal albatross. Viewing by appointment only. The centre is open all year, but chicks are on the nests from the end of January through to the end of August.
- Yellow-eyed penguin Conservation Reserve, Otago Peninsula, Dunedin.
- Black Stilt Viewing Hide, Twizel.
- Takahe aviaries, Te Anau. The takahe was considered extinct until its rediscovery in Fiordland in 1948.
- Stewart Island is a haven for many native bird species, including the southern tokoeka, the only species of kiwi active during the day.

- The only bird in the world whose beak twists entirely to one side is the New Zealand wrybill.
- The Forest and Bird website (www.forest-bird.org.nz) gives a list of good places to watch New Zealand birds.

Bird extinctions, mostly after human arrival (c. AD 1000)

Adzebill
Chatham Island duck
Chatham Island sea-eagle (overlap with humans unknown)
De Lautour's duck (probably pre-human extinction)
Eyles' harrier
Finsch's duck
Giant Chatham Island rail
Giant Chatham Island snipe
Grant-Mackie's/North Island stout-legged wren (overlap with humans unknown)
Hodgen's rail
Moa (11 species)
New Zealand coot
New Zealand crow
New Zealand owlet-nightjar (overlap with humans unknown)
New Zealand pelican (overlap with humans unknown)
New Zealand swan
North Island goose
North Island takahe (subspecies)
Scarlett's duck (pre-human extinction)
Snipe-rail
South Island goose
Te pouakai or Te hokioi/Haast's or New Zealand eagle
Yaldwyn's/South Island stout-legged wren (overlap with humans unknown)

Bird extinctions after European arrival (from AD 1800)

Auckland Island merganser
Bush wren
Chatham Island bellbird (subspecies)
Chatham Island fernbird
Chatham Island rail
Dieffenbach's rail (flightless subspecies of the banded rail)
Huia
Koreke/New Zealand quail
Little Barrier snipe (subspecies)
New Zealand little bittern
New Zealand storm-petrel
North Island piopio
South Island piopio
Stephen's Island wren
Tutukiwi/Stewart Island snipe (subspecies)
Whekau/laughing owl

- The deathblow to the huia was the gift of a huia feather to the visiting Duke of York. This simple act increased the demand for huia feathers a hundredfold.
- One lighthouse keeper's cat eliminated all the Stephen's Island wrens soon after the species was discovered.

'Nationally Critical' birds

Black robin
Black stilt
Campbell Island snipe
Campbell Island teal
Chatham Island oystercatcher
Chatham Island pigeon, parea
Codfish Island fernbird, matata
Codfish Island South Georgian diving petrel

Common noddy
Crested grebe
Fairy tern
Haast tokoeka (kiwi)
Kakapo
Kermadec white-faced storm petrel
Masked booby
New Zealand shore plover, tutu
Okarito brown kiwi
Orange-fronted parakeet
South Island brown teal
South Island kokako (probably extinct)
Southern New Zealand dotterel
Taiko
Takahe
White heron
White tern

The South Island kokako is probably extinct, although there have been 60 reported sightings in 10 years, mainly on the West Coast and the western foothills and hinterland of Canterbury.

Numbers of further species and subspecies of birds at risk

- Nationally Endangered: 22
- Nationally Vulnerable: 9
- Serious Decline: 8
- Gradual Decline: 20
- Sparse: 11
- Range Restricted: 50

There are four species of kiwi, and six identified varieties. The total numbers of kiwi are estimated at 85,000, and these are declining in the North and South Islands by about 5.8% a year, or halving every decade.

Interbreeding between the introduced mallard duck and the native grey duck is creating an extensive hybrid population, the grallard, and threatening the existence of the grey duck.

Mammals

Before the arrival of humans, the only land-dwelling mammals in New Zealand were bats. Polynesians brought two mammals to New Zealand: the Polynesian rat, kiore, and dog, kuri. Europeans then brought many more. All introduced mammals have had a huge impact on the native species of New Zealand, and have been the main cause of extinctions in native plants and animals since human arrival (along with human activity).

Native mammals: bats

- **New Zealand long-tailed bat (pekapeka):** This bat has a membrane attached to the full length of its tail which is used to scoop up insects while on the wing. It is an endemic species, but other members of the same bat family are found in nearby countries. The South Island long-tailed bat is listed as being 'Nationally Endangered', and the North Island long-tailed bat is 'Nationally Vulnerable'.
- **New Zealand lesser short-tailed bat:** This is an ancient species unique to New Zealand, found only at a few scattered sites. It is a 'species of the highest conservation value', especially as it is the only remaining species of a family of bats found only in New Zealand. These bats are adapted to ground hunting and spend large amounts of time on the forest floor, using their folded wings as 'front limbs' for scrambling around.

  The northern short-tailed bat and the southern short-tailed bat are both listed as 'Nationally Endangered.'

  The New Zealand greater short-tailed bat was found on two islands off Stewart Island, but following an invasion of ship rats, it was last sighted in the mid-1960s and is probably extinct.

The Australian little red flying fox bat has been occasionally blown to New Zealand but has not survived here.

Marine mammals

All seals, whales and dolphins are protected under the Marine Mammals Protection Act 1978.

Seals

Two families of seals are found in the New Zealand region:

- **Sea lions and fur seals (eared seals):**
  Hooker's/New Zealand sea lion
  New Zealand fur seal
- **True seals:**
  Crabeater seal
  Leopard seal (sea leopard)
  Ross seal (only rarely reach the subantarctic islands)
  Southern elephant seal/sea elephant
  Weddell seal

- The Hooker's sea lion is New Zealand's only endemic seal. Total population is relatively small (5000–7000).
- Seals can be dangerous, especially as their bites can cause agonising infections in humans. Early sealers were known to have tried to cut off body parts affected by septic seal bites.

Whales, dolphins and porpoises

There are six families of cetaceans found in New Zealand waters.

Baleen whales

Rorquals

Blue whale (the largest whale, up to 30 m and over 120 tonnes)
Bryde's whale
Fin whale
Humpback whale (the most common in New Zealand waters, reaching 15 m in length)
Minke whale
Sei whale

Right whales

Pygmy right whale
Southern right whale

Baleen whales have no teeth, but use horny baleen plates to filter food from sea water.

Toothed whales

Sperm whales

Dwarf sperm whale
Pygmy sperm whale
Sperm whale

Beaked whales

Andrews' beaked whale
Arnoux's beaked whale
Ginkgo-toothed whale
Goose-beaked whale
Hector's beaked whale
Scamperdown whale
Shepherd's beaked whale
Southern bottlenose whale
Strap-toothed whale

Pilot whales, which swim in large groups, are most likely to have mass strandings.

Dolphins

Bottlenose dolphin
Common dolphin
Long-finned pilot whale
Melon-headed whale

Dusky dolphin
False killer whale
Hector's dolphin
Hourglass dolphin
Orca (killer whale)
Porpoises
Spectacled porpoise

Risso's dolphin
Short-finned pilot whale
Southern right whale dolphin
Spotted dolphin
Striped dolphin

The 1.4 m Hector's dolphin, also known as the 'downunder dolphin' because it is found only in New Zealand waters, is one of the smallest and rarest in the world. Genetic studies have shown that the species consists of three, most likely four, distinct populations that do not interbreed.

Famous New Zealand dolphins

- Pelorus Jack (a Risso's dolphin) guided ships from Wellington to Nelson from 1888 to 1912.
- Opo (a bottlenose dolphin) played with children in Opononi in Hokianga Harbour in the summer of 1955–56.
- Maui (a bottlenose) from 1992–94 played with divers and boaties around Kaikoura and the Marlborough Sounds.

Some places to view whales and dolphins

- The Kaikoura coast: sperm whales and dusky dolphins.
- The Hauraki Gulf: common and bottlenose dolphins.
- The Sugar Loaf Islands Marine Reserve: common and Hector's dolphins, killer, pilot and humpback whales.
- Milford Sound: bottlenose dolphins.

Endangered marine mammals

'Nationally Critical' marine mammals include:

Bryde's whale
Orca (killer whale)

North Island Hector's dolphin
Southern elephant seal

There are less than 100 North Island Hector's dolphin left.

Introduced wild or feral mammals

Marsupials	
Black-tailed/swamp wallaby	c. 1870, by Sir George Grey, on Kawau Island, Hauraki Gulf.
Black-striped wallaby (now very rare or extinct)	c. 1870, by Sir George Grey, on Kawau Island.
Brush-tailed rock wallaby	1873, by J. Reid, on Motutapu Island, Hauraki Gulf.
Common brushtail possum/ possum	First unsuccessful release c. 1838. First successful release 1858, near Riverton. 1890–1900 many Australian possums released by acclimatisation societies. 1890–1940 (especially) more liberations of NZ-born possums.
Red-necked/Bennett's wallaby	1874, near Waimate in Canterbury.
Tammar/dama wallaby	c. 1870, by Sir George Grey, on Kawau Island.
White-throated/ Parma wallaby	c. 1870, by Sir George Grey, on Kawau Island.
Insectivores	
Hedgehog	First recorded 1870.
Lagomorphs	
Brown hare	1851 first swam ashore, followed soon after by human-assisted liberations.
Rabbit	1777, by James Cook, on Motuara Island in Queen Charlotte Sound.
Rodents	
House mouse	1824 recorded date of first mouse stowaways/escapees, from a shipwreck on Ruapuke Island in Foveaux Strait.
Kiore/Polynesian rat	c. AD 1000 with first Polynesians.

Norway rat	Late 18th century, or perhaps even 1772, as escapees from whaling and sealing ships.
Ship rat	1850s onwards, as Norway rats were dominant on visiting ships from 1700 until 1850.
Carnivores	
Feral cat	From 1769 onwards as all ships carried cats to counter rat infestation. Feral cats were observed some 50 years later.
Feral ferret	1879, as anti-rabbit agents.
Kuri/Maori dog	c. AD 900 as domestic animals.
Stoat	1884, as anti-rabbit agents.
Weasel	1885, as anti-rabbit agents.
Odd-toed ungulates	
Feral horse	1814 brought by Samuel Marsden to Bay of Islands. Feral horses recorded in Kaimanawa ranges by 1876.
Even-toed ungulates	
Chamois	1907 as a gift from the Emperor Franz Josef of Austria.
Fallow deer	1860 to 1910 at least 24 successful liberations.
Feral cattle	1814 brought by Samuel Marsden to Bay of Islands. By 1819 wild cattle reported.
Feral goat	1773, by Captain Cook.
Feral pig/Captain Cookers/ kunekune	1769 the French explorer De Surville presented two pigs to Maori at Doubtless Bay, Northland, which did not survive. 1773 Captain Cook released pigs.

Feral sheep	Sheep introduced throughout 19th century, some of which became feral.
Himalayan tahr	1904 by NZ government for hunting, gifted from Duke of Bedford.
Moose	1910 first successful liberation (1900 liberation died out.). No confirmed sightings over the last 40 years.
Red deer	1851: about 1000 released by 1923.
Rusa deer	1907, accidentally imported as 'sambar deer'.
Sambar deer	1875, single pair imported from Sri Lanka.
Sika deer	1905 first successful liberation, gifted by Duke of Bedford. (1885 liberation probably shot by settlers.)
Wapiti	1905 first successful liberation (1870s unsuccessful liberation). Interbreed with red deer.
White-tailed deer	1905 first successful liberation. (1901 liberation unsuccessful.)

Notes:

1. There are no pure-bred kuri left, as they interbred with European dogs.
2. The introduction of stoats and weasels to kill rabbits in the 19th century was opposed by ornithologists, whose fears that they would also kill birds were sadly proved correct.
3. Humans arrived c. 1000 years ago, and have had the greatest impact upon the New Zealand ecology since the Ice Ages.

In New Zealand, cats are the most popular domestic pets with 47% of households owning at least one cat. The country's cat per human population is one of the highest in the world, and New Zealanders keep around four or five times more cats than dogs.

Reptiles and amphibians

The reptiles and amphibians found in New Zealand are tuatara, lizards (skinks and geckos) and frogs. The tuatara and New Zealand frogs are particularly ancient creatures, whose nearest relatives are known to us only through fossils.

Tuatara

The tuatara (Maori for spiny back) is the only living member of the ancient family of Rhynchocephalia (beak-headed reptiles), which flourished around 200 million years ago. All other members of the family died out around 100 million years ago.

- Total number estimated at around 100,000.
- About half live on islands in Cook Strait and the rest are spread over islands around the top half of the North Island.
- There are two species of tuatara.
  - The most common species is found on the northern islands. It is thought that the Cook Strait islands tuatara is a subspecies of this northern tuatara.
  - Another species lives on one tiny island in Cook Strait.
- Tuatara are basically nocturnal.
- Food is mainly beetles, worms, snails, weta and sometimes seabird eggs and chicks.
- Tuatara breed only every two to four years.
- Tuatara lay about a dozen leathery-shelled eggs between October and December. The eggs are burrowed and then abandoned.
- After about 12–15 months the eggs hatch, with the sex of the babies depending on soil temperature. (As with crocodiles and turtles, warmer temperatures produce predominantly males and cooler temperatures females.)
- Adults can grow up to 24 cm in length and weigh about 500 g.
- Tuatara mature at about 13 years old and may live to be 60 years old.

Places to see tuatara

- Somes Island in Wellington Harbour
- Auckland Zoo
- Mt Bruce National Wildlife Centre
- Southland Museum
- There is a proposal to relocate some tuatara on the Hauraki Gulf's open sanctuary, Tiritiri Matangi Island, so that more people can see tuatara in their natural habitat.

Lizards

New Zealand has two families of lizards: geckos and skinks. Nearly all bear their young live rather than laying eggs. This is thought to be a cool-weather adaptation.

New Zealand has the only live-bearing geckos in the world.

Geckos	Skinks
Dull or velvety loose-fitting skin.	Shiny and smooth skin.
Scales small and granular.	Skin has overlapping scales.
Skin sloughs off in once piece.	Skin sloughs off piecemeal.
Large eyes with oval catlike pupils, fixed eyelids. Wider, rather frog-like heads.	Small eyes with small round pupils and moveable eyelids. Pointed rather snake-like heads.
Mostly nocturnal.	Mostly active during the day.
More slow moving.	Darting speed.
Most species arboreal. (tree dwellers)	Most species terrestrial (ground dwellers).

Both shed their tails to help them escape from predators.

Geckos

- There are two main groups of New Zealand geckos: the *Hoplodactylus* (grey-brown, 22 species) and the *Naultinas* (green, seven species).

- Gecko species are still being discovered and classified. As recently as 1998 a striking gecko with orange patches was found on Mt Roy near Wanaka.
- Geckos can walk up glass and even upside down on ceilings, due to the very complex structure of their feet.
- A gecko's eyeball is completely covered by a transparent lid, which is why they can lick their eyes.
- Some New Zealand geckos use their tail as a prehensile fifth leg.
- Unlike many other reptiles, geckos can make sounds.
- The Maori dreaded the green gecko (moko kakariki) as a symbol of disaster.

Skinks

- New Zealand has 28 species of skink.
- Skink eyes have two lids. The upper lid is fixed, but the lower is movable and has a transparent 'window', which protects it from dust.
- New Zealand has only one species of egg-laying skink.
- The common skink and the copper skink are the most common New Zealand skinks.
- The Otago skink is the largest mainland skink.
- Skinks are found from the seaside to the mountain tops, but their numbers have been greatly reduced by introduced mammal predators.
- One feral cat can kill thousands of skinks each year.

The only two occasions when snakes were officially allowed into New Zealand were in 1905 and 1907 with vaudeville entertainer, Cleopatra, who performed with snakes, alligators and crocodiles.

Endangered reptiles

'Nationally Critical' reptiles

Open Bay Islands skink
Open Bay Islands gecko
Roys Peak gecko
Takitimus gecko

'Nationally Endangered' reptiles

Brothers Island tuatara
Chevron skink
Grand skink
Otago skink

Frogs

New Zealand's native frogs belong to the genus *Leiopelma*, an ancient and primitive group of frogs. The frogs have changed very little in 70 million years. They are small, nocturnal and are hard to see as they are well camouflaged. Three of our remaining species live on land in shady, moist forested areas, and one is semi-aquatic, living on stream edges.

New Zealand originally had seven species of native frog. Three species have become extinct since the arrival of humans and animal pests. The four remaining species are:

- **Hochstetter's frog**: The most widespread native frog, although it is still listed as 'Sparse'. It lives on sites around the upper half of the North Island, grows up to 48 mm long, has partially webbed feet, more warts than the other frogs, and is generally dark brown.
- **Archey's frog:** This is found only in the Coromandel and in one site west of Te Kuiti. It is the smallest native frog, growing up to 37 mm long. It lives in misty, moist areas around 400 m in altitude. It is listed as 'Nationally Critical'.
- **Hamilton's frog:** This is also 'Nationally Critical' as it is one of the world's most endangered frogs. It is found only on one island in Cook Strait. It is the largest native frog.
- **Maud Island frog:** This species were found on Maud Island in the Marlborough Sounds, although recently

DOC transferred some Maud Island frogs to another Marlborough Sounds island. It is listed as 'Nationally Endangered'.

Frogs are declining everywhere in the world. Fungal disease is probably the cause of the highly endangered status of Archey's frog.

New Zealand's native frogs have several distinctive features, which make them very different from frogs elsewhere in the world:

- They have no external eardrum.
- They have round (not slit) eyes.
- They don't croak regularly like most frogs.
- They don't have a tadpole stage. The embryo develops inside an egg, and then hatches as an almost fully formed frog. The young of most species are cared for by their parents; e.g. the male Archey's frog may carry his young offspring around on his back.

There are also three introduced species of frog in New Zealand. These species are easily distinguished from native frogs because they have loud mating calls and pass through a tadpole stage. They are:

- Brown tree or whistling frog
- Green and golden bell frog
- Southern bell frog

Fish

Freshwater fish

- There are 56 species of true freshwater fish in New Zealand. (Another seven essentially marine species sometimes enter fresh water.)
- 35 freshwater fish species are native.

- 21 are introduced. (Some of the introduced fish, such as koi carp, are pests that destroy habitats and compete with or feed on native fish.)
- Native New Zealand fish tend to be small, secretive, nocturnal and well camouflaged.
- Galaxids are the largest family of freshwater fish, with 13 species. The seasonal delicacy,whitebait, are juvenile galaxids.
- New Zealand has three native species of mudfish which aestivate for up to five months in the summer (to aestivate is the summer equivalent of hibernating in the winter). Mudfish can burrow up to a metre down into the ground.
- Salmon were introduced in 1868 but were not properly established until 1921.
- Trout were introduced in the 1860s and are now a mix of varieties from Europe.

The lamprey looks like an eel, but is a primitive fish that feeds upon marine fish and whales by clamping onto them with its circle of small, horny teeth. Lamprey come into fresh water to spawn, and then die.

Endangered freshwater fish

'Nationally Critical': Kakanui longjaw

'Nationally Endangered': Canterbury mudfish; Northland mudfish

Eels

- There are three species of freshwater eels in New Zealand, one of which seems to be only a recent but successful immigrant from Australia.
- The long-finned and short-finned eels migrate to the tropical Pacific to spawn and die, after years in fresh water.
- Eels can live for many years. A 10 kg eel could be 60–70

years old. Some eels reach as long as at least 1.75 m and weigh 24 kg.

- There are also saltwater eels, such as the moray and conger eels.
- Eels were an important food source for Maori, and are now a commercially farmed species.

Marine fish

New Zealand's Exclusive Economic Zone control over its seas is the fourth largest in the world. In this zone there are more than 1000 species of fish. Some live throughout the world's seas, some occur in the Australian, Indian Ocean and Antarctic waters and a few are endemic to New Zealand waters.

Endemic species are mainly fish that live in rock pools, for example the cockabullies. Blue cod is another endemic fish.

Marine fish habitats

The main habitats of New Zealand marine fish and sample fish species are:

- Estuaries: flounder, sole, spotties, stingrays; and school sharks and snapper (as breeding grounds).
- Sandy shores: flounder, sole, red gurnard.
- Rocky coastlines and rock pools: blennies, kelpfish, butterfish, wrasse, red moki, tarakihi.
- Offshore reefs (up to 150 m deep): conger and moray eels, rock cod, sea perch, blue maomao, leatherjacket, demoiselles, bass grouper, sharks, barracouta, kingfish, jack mackerels.
- Continental shelf (up to 200 m deep): hoki, hake, gemfish, silver and white warehou, silver and orange roughies, tuna.
- Ocean waters (up to several km deep): viperfish, black dragon fish, marlin, sharks.

Invertebrates

Invertebrates are a hugely diverse group, ranging from spiders and jellyfish to worms and weta. They are extremely important to all life on earth as they recycle nutrients, maintain soil structure, pollinate plants and provide food for other animals.

Many of New Zealand's invertebrate species are ancient, of Gondwana origins. Many are also struggling to survive against recently introduced predators. DOC has classed 280 species as conservation priorities, and listed another 540 which could also be in danger. Twelve marine invertebrates, including three species of octopus, are in the 'Nationally Critical' endangered category.

Many New Zealand bird lice are highly endangered, due to the rarity of their hosts. Similarly there is a moth that feeds on guano of short-tailed bats which is listed as 'Nationally Critical'. The extinction of one species can be the catalyst for many more.

Some invertebrate facts

- New Zealand has 24 butterfly species but more than 1500 species of moth.
- The puriri or ghost moth is New Zealand's largest endemic moth. The larger female has a wingspan of 150 mm.
- The huhu is New Zealand's largest beetle, and its grubs were considered a delicacy by the Maori, once the grubs had finished feeding.
- There are 30 species of stick insect endemic to New Zealand.
- Only the female sandfly sucks blood, and is most active at dawn and dusk. Only two species bite humans, one species bites penguins, and the remaining eight of 11 endemic species probably bite other birds. New Zealand sandflies do not transmit diseases.

- New Zealand mosquitoes are harmless to humans.
- Weta are part of New Zealand's ancient species from Gondwana. They belong to the grasshopper family, are wingless, and have ears on their front legs. The largest weta is the wetapunga, 82 mm long, which lives on Great Barrier Island.
- New Zealand has more than 1000 species of snails, from the tiny to the huge 75 mm kauri snails. Most snails are vegetarian, but some are carnivorous.
- *Rhytida* snails eat other snails by biting off their heads, and then digesting their bodies by inserting their tails into their prey's shell and secreting digestive fluid. Even the eaten snail's shell is dissolved and absorbed.
- The peripatus is an ancient creature that resembles 500 million-year-old fossils. It has the features of both annelid worms and arthropods.

Spiders

Zoologists estimate there may be 2500 species of spiders in New Zealand, of which only 500 have been 'described'. A recent and rapidly spreading newcomer is the white-tail spider, which is poisonous but not deadly to humans.

The katipo spider is New Zealand's only dangerously poisonous creature. It is found most frequently on the western beaches of the North Island. Its bite can be fatal, but only two deaths from a katipo bite have been recorded, both in the 19th century. Today there is an antivenom to the bite.

National parks and reserves

About 8 million ha (nearly 30%) of New Zealand land is managed as conservation land, mostly by the Department of Conservation (DOC). DOC also has responsibility for the preservation and management of wildlife, and has a role in management of the coastal marine area.

Conservation areas

14 national parks	3 million ha (just over 10% NZ land mass)
20 conservation (forest) parks	1.8 million ha
3500 reserves	1.5 million ha approx.
Other DOC-managed conservation areas	2.8 million ha approx.
Protected private land	61,000 ha
Marine reserves	1.1 million ha

Marine reserves

- There are 16 marine reserves. The Kermadec Islands Marine Reserve is the largest at 748,000 ha.
- There are two marine mammal sanctuaries: the Banks Peninsula and Auckland Islands Marine Mammal Sanctuaries.
- There are three marine parks: Mimiwhangata, Tawharanui and the Hauraki Gulf Marine Park.
- The Sugar Loaf Islands are a marine protected area.

Fiordland National Park is the largest national park in New Zealand and one of the largest in the world.

National parks

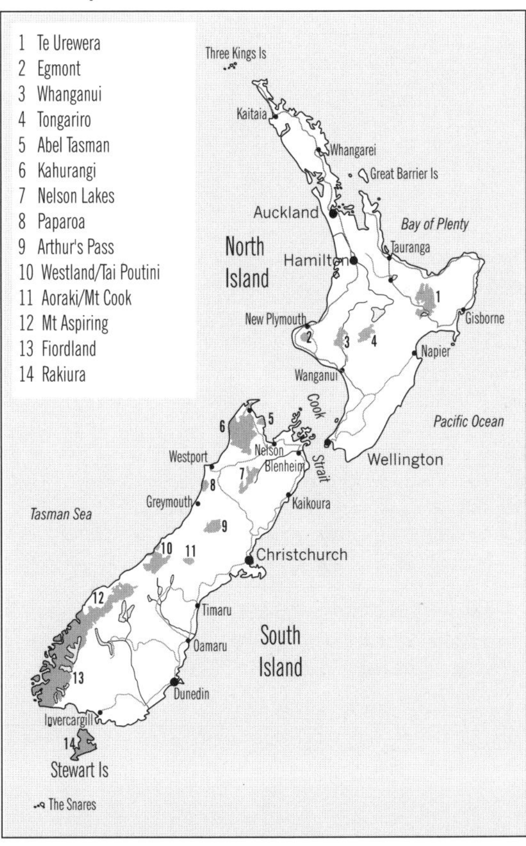

National parks (from north to south; size [ha] and date established)

Tongariro	79 598	1887
Te Urewera	212 675	1954
Egmont	33 543	1900
Whanganui	74 231	1986
Kahurangi	452 000	1996
Abel Tasman	22 541	1942
Nelson Lakes	101 753	1956
Paparoa	30 560	1987
Arthur's Pass	114 357	1929
Westland/Tai Poutini	117 547	1960
Aoraki/Mount Cook	70 696	1953
Mount Aspiring	355 531	1964
Fiordland	1 251 924	1952
Rakiura	157 000	2000

New Zealand has three world heritage area sites:

- Te Wahipounamu (south-west New Zealand, incorporating Fiordland).
- Tongariro National Park.
- The New Zealand Sub-Antarctic Islands Reserve (approximately 74,885 ha, made up of the Snares Islands, Auckland Islands, Campbell Island, Antipodes Island and Bounty Islands).

Tongariro National Park was the first national park in the world to be freely gifted to the nation by an indigenous people, the Ngati Tuwharetoa, to whom its mountains are sacred.

Great Walks of New Zealand

Abel Tasman Coastal Track
Heaphy Track
Kepler Track
Lake Waikaremoana Track
Milford Track
Rakiura Track
Routeburn Track
Tongariro Northern Circuit
Whanganui Journey

The 'Great Walks' are several-day hikes through the national parks. They are maintained and controlled by DOC. (See the DOC website at the back of the book for information on the walks and parks.)

Conservation issues

Conservation issues are discussed in Section 3: Resources and Economy. This is because conservation issues and the state of the environment cannot be seen separately from the human activities that threaten or support them.

SECTION 2
People

History
100 important events

1.	c. 1300	Polynesian settlement known to be established by this date (first arrivals earlier).
2.	1642	Dutch explorer Abel Tasman discovers 'Staten Landt', later named 'Nieuw Zeeland'.
3.	1769	British explorer James Cook's first of three visits, claiming New Zealand for England's George III.
4.	1790s	Sealing, deep-sea whaling, the flax and timber trades begin; small temporary settlements.
5.	1814	Anglican mission established, Rangihoua, Bay of Islands.
6.	1815	First European child born in New Zealand.
7.	1820	Hongi Hika, Ngapuhi chief, visits England, meets King George IV and secures supply of muskets.
8.	1821	Musket wars (intertribal) begin and continue throughout the decade.
9.	1822	Wesleyan mission established at Whangaroa.
10.	1827	Te Rauparaha's invasion of the South Island.
11.	1835	Declaration of Independence by the 'United Tribes of New Zealand' signed by 34 northern chiefs.
12.	1838	Bishop Pompallier founds Roman Catholic Mission at Hokianga.
13.	1839	William Hobson instructed to establish British rule in New Zealand, as a dependency of New South Wales.

14.	1840	Wellington settlement.
15.		Treaty of Waitangi signed.
16.	1844	Hone Heke begins the 'War in the North'.
17.	1846	'War in the North' ends.
18.	1848	Otago settlement. Main South Island purchase.
19.	1854	First session of the General Assembly opens in Auckland.
20.	1860	Taranaki land dispute develops into the beginning of the Land Wars.
21.	1861	Otago goldrushes begin.
22.	1863	War resumes in Taranaki and begins in Waikato.
23.		First steam railway.
24.	1864	War in the Waikato ends.
25.		West Coast goldrush.
26.	1865	Native Land Court established.
27.	1867	Thames goldrush.
28.		Four Maori seats established in Parliament.
29.	1868	Maori resistance continues through campaigns of Te Kooti Arikirangi and Titokowaru.
30.	1869	New Zealand's first university, the University of Otago, established at Dunedin.
31.	1870	Vogel announces national railway construction programme: over 1000 miles constructed by 1879.
32.	1872	Maori armed resistance ceases.
33.	1876	New Zealand-Australia telegraph cable established.
34.	1877	Education Act establishes free, compulsory, secular education.
35.	1879	Vote is given to every male aged 21 and over.
36.	1882	First shipment of frozen meat to Britain.
37.	1883	Direct steamer link to Britain.
38.	1886	Mt Tarawera erupts, killing over 100 people, and destroying the famous Pink and White Terraces.

39.	1887	Reefton becomes first town to have electricity.
40.	1890	First election on a one-man one-vote basis.
41.	1893	Women allowed to vote in national election.
42.	1898	Old Age Pensions Act (first of its kind in the world).
43.	1899	New Zealand army contingent is sent to the South African War.
44.	1901	Cook and other Pacific Islands annexed.
45.	1904	Richard Pearse achieves semi-controlled flight near Timaru.
46.	1905	New Zealand rugby team tours England, becomes known as the All Blacks.
47.	1907	New Zealand constituted as a Dominion.
48.	1908	Ernest Rutherford is awarded the Nobel Prize in Chemistry.
49.		New Zealand's population reaches 1 million.
50.	1914	First World War begins and German Samoa is occupied by New Zealand.
51.	1915	New Zealand forces take part in the Gallipoli campaign.
52.	1916	Labour Party formed.
53.	1917	Battle of Passchendaele: 3700 New Zealanders killed.
54.	1918	End of First World War.
55.		Worldwide influenza epidemic kills an estimated 8500 people in New Zealand.
56.	1919	Women eligible for election to Parliament.
57.	1926	National public broadcasting begins.
58.	1929	Economic depression worsens.
59.	1931	Napier earthquake kills 256.
60.	1936	State housing programme launched.
61.		National Party formed from former Coalition MPs.

62.	1938	Social Security Act establishes revised pensions structure and the basis of a national health service.
63.	1939	Second World War begins. Second New Zealand Expeditionary Force formed. Bulk purchases of farm products by Great Britain.
64.	1945	War in Europe ends on 8 May and in the Pacific on 15 August.
65.		National Airways Corporation founded.
66.	1947	Full independence from Britain.
67.	1950	Naval and ground forces sent to Korean War.
68.		Wool boom begins.
69.	1951	Prolonged waterfront dispute; state of emergency proclaimed.
70.		ANZUS Treaty signed between United States, Australia and New Zealand.
71.	1952	Population reaches over 2 million.
72.	1953	New Zealander Edmund Hillary and Sherpa Tenzing Norgay first to climb Mount Everest.
73.	1959	Auckland harbour bridge opened.
74.	1960	Regular television programmes begin in Auckland.
75.	1961	Capital punishment abolished.
76.	1962	Western Samoa becomes independent.
77.	1965	New Zealand combat force sent to Vietnam; protest movement begins.
78.		The Cook Islands become self-governing.
79.	1967	Decimal currency introduced.
80.	1969	Vote extended to 20 year olds.
81.	1975	The Waitangi Tribunal established.
82.	1976	Introduction of metric system of weights and measures.
83.	1977	National Superannuation scheme begins.

84. 1977 The 200-mile exclusive economic zone established in the seas around New Zealand.

85. 1979 An Air New Zealand DC10-30 crashes into Mt Erebus, Antarctica, killing all 257 onboard.

86. 1981 South African rugby team's tour brings widespread disruption.

87. 1982 Closer Economic Relations agreement signed with Australia.

88. 1984 Labour Party wins snap General Election. Finance Minister Roger Douglas begins deregulating the economy.

89. 1985 Anti-nuclear policy leads to refusal of a visit by an American warship.

90. Greenpeace vessel *Rainbow Warrior* bombed and sunk by French agents in Auckland harbour.

91. Waitangi Tribunal given power to hear grievances arising since 1840.

92. 1986 Homosexual Law Reform Bill passed.

93. Goods and Services Tax introduced.

94. 1987 Share prices plummet by 59% in four months.

95. 1990 Welfare payments cut.

96. 1991 Employment Contracts Act passed.

97. 1996 First MMP election brings National/New Zealand First coalition Government.

98. 1997 Jim Bolger is replaced by New Zealand's first woman Prime Minister, Jenny Shipley.

99. 1999 Labour leader Helen Clark becomes the first elected woman Prime Minister, in minority coalition with the Alliance party.

100. 2000 Country celebrates the new millennium.

Coming ashore: waves of immigration

New Zealand immigration has had three main phases:

- Maori, from East Polynesia.
- Europeans in early 19th and most of 20th centuries.
- Many sources, including the Pacific Islands and Asia, especially since the 1960s.

The origins of immigrants to New Zealand began to change after 1987. New legislation then favoured the skills and resources brought by immigrants, not their country of origin.

Some peoples and approximate arrival dates

Maori	c. 1000 (debated)
Germans	1834, Nelson
English	1840, at Port Nicholson, Wellington
French	1840, at Akaroa, Canterbury
Jews	1840s
Scottish	1848, Otago
Hungry Young Men (of many nations, mainly British and Irish)	1861, start of the Otago goldrushes
Scandinavians	1860s, Manawatu
Chinese	late 1860s, to Otago goldfields, 1990s on
Irish	1870s assisted emigration schemes
Dalmatians	1880s on, to the kauri gumfields of Northland
Lebanese	1890s
European anti-Fascists	1930s (small numbers)
Indians	1930s (some Sikhs from the Punjab from 1890s), 1990s on

Polish	1950s, 6000 Second World War refugees (also earlier group in 1870s)
Dutch	early 1950s
Hungarians	1956 revolution refugees (about 1000)
Pacific Islanders	1960s, 1970s, and again in late 1980s
Sri Lankans	1970s to present
Vietnamese, Cambodians, Laotians	1975 to present: 7000 refugees
Chileans, Russian Jews, East Europeans, Assyrians, Ethiopians, Iraqis, Bosnians, Somalians, Afghanis	1970s to present: small numbers of refugees
Fijian Indians	After 1987 coup in Fiji
Hong Kong citizens	1990s onwards
Taiwanese	1990s onwards
Koreans	1990s onwards
South Africans	1990s onwards
Middle Eastern peoples	1990s onwards
North African peoples	1990s onwards

The first Europeans to live in New Zealand were a sealing gang left in Dusky Sound, Fiordland, in 1792.

Pacific Island peoples

- There is special provision for immigration from Western Samoa under the Treaty of Friendship signed in 1962 when Samoa gained independence from New Zealand.
- People from the Cook Islands, Niue and the Tokelau Islands are all New Zealand citizens with the right of free entry into New Zealand.

The first attempt at British colonisation was in 1825. However, only four of 60 immigrants aboard the *Rosanna* stayed.

Some commonly agreed European firsts

First Dutchman	Abel Tasman, 1642
First Englishman	James Cook, 1769
First Frenchman	De Surville, two months after Cook (still 1769)
First Spaniard	Malaspina, 1793

Iwi (Maori tribes)

Iwi is the largest social group within Maoridom. Each iwi is divided into hapu (sub-tribes), which in turn are made up of whanau (households). Maori communities and their structure have often changed, however, so that some hapu may become dominant within an iwi.

Membership of an iwi is dependent on descent from a common ancestor, as with a hapu. A group of tribes trace their ancestry to those who arrived in one of the immigrant waka (canoes).

Iwi and their arrival canoes (from which descent is traced)

Northern (Tai-Tokerau)

1. Aupouri	Kurahaupo and others
2. Rarawa	Kurahaupo and others
3. Ngati Kahu	Kurahaupo and others
4. Ngapuhi	Kurahaupo and others
5. Ngati Whatua	Kurahaupo and others

Tainui	
6. Ngati Tai	Tainui
7. Ngati Paoa	Tainui
8. Ngati Maru	Tainui
9. Ngati Tamatera	Tainui
10. Ngati Whanaunga	Tainui
11. Waikato	Tainui
12. Maniapoto	Tainui
Taranaki	
13. Ngati Tama	Tokomaru
14. Ngati Mutunga	Tokomaru
15. Ngati Maru	Tokomaru
16. Te Ati Awa	Tokomaru
17. Taranaki	Kurahaupo
18. Nga Ruahine	Aotea
19. Ngati Ruanui	Aotea
20. Nga Rauru	Aotea
Wanganui	
21. Ngati Haua	Tainui and Arawa
22. Te Ati Hau	Aotea and Kurahaupo
Manawatu	
23. Ngati Ruakawa	Tainui
24. Ngati Apa	Kurahaupo
25. Rangitane	Kurahaupo
26. Muaupoko	Kurahaupo

Wellington	
16. Te Ati Awa	Tokomaru
27. Ngati Toa	Tainui
Arawa iwi	
28. Arawa	Arawa
29. Ngati Tuwharetoa	Arawa
Bay of Plenty iwi	
30. Ngai Terangi	Mataatua and Tainui
31. Ngati Ranginui	Mataatua and Tainui
32. Ngati Awa	Mataatua
33. Tuhoe	Mataatua
34. Whakatohea	Mataatua
35. Ngai Tai	Tainui
36. Whanau-a-Apanui	Mataatua and Horouta
East Coast (Tai-Rawhiti)	
37. Ngati Porou	Horouta
38. Rongowhakaata	Takitimu
39. Te Aitanga-a-Mahaki	Takitimu
Takitimu	
40. Ngati Kahungunu	Takitimu
25. Rangitane	Kurahaupo
South Island	
13. Ngati Tama	Tokomaru
14. Ngati Mutunga	Tokomaru
16. Te Ati Awa	Tokomaru

25. Rangitane	Kurahaupo
27. Ngati Toa	Tainui
41. Poutini	Takitimu and others
42. Ngai Tahu/Kai Tahu	Takitimu and others
42a. Ngati Mamoe*	Takitimu and others

*Ngai Mamoe of the southern South Island were completely assimilated by the invading Ngai Tahu in the 18th and 19th centuries. Today Ngati Mamoe and the southern Ngai Tahu are virtually one people.

Iwi affiliation

One in six people (604,110) are of Maori descent. (Descent is a different concept to that of ethnicity, which is related to cultural identification.)

Largest iwi (2001 and 1991 Counts)

Ngapuhi	102 981	92 976
Ngati Porou	61 701	48 525
Ngai Tahu/Kai Tahu	39 180	20 304

Iwi with populations over 10,000 (in order of descending size)

Ngapuhi
Ngati Porou
Ngai Tahu/Kai Tahu
Waikato
Ngati Tawharetoa
Tuhoe
Ngati Maniapoto
Ngati Kahungunu (region unspecified)
Te Arawa
Ngati Kahungunu (ki Te Wairoa)
Ngati Awa

Tainui
Ngati Whatua
Te Rarawa
Ngati Raukawa (Horowhenua/Manawatu)
Te Arawa (Taupo Region)
Te Atiawa (Taranaki)

Moriori

The Moriori people lived on the Chatham Islands/Rekohu and had renounced warfare. All disputes were settled by duel using a stick of a thumb's thickness and an arm's length; the winner was the first to draw blood. Most of the Moriori were killed or enslaved when the Ngati Tama and Ngati Mutunga of the Wairarapa arrived in 1835, although more than 2000 people today can trace their ancestry to the Moriori.

The Treaty of Waitangi

The Treaty of Waitangi is seen as the founding document of the nation of New Zealand. It was signed in 1840 by representatives of the British Crown and Maori chiefs.

By signing the Treaty, the chiefs relinquished their sovereignty in exchange for the 'exclusive and undisturbed possession of the Lands and Estates, Forests, Fisheries and other properties' unless they wished to sell them. In exchange, Maori received the protection of the Queen and 'all the rights and privileges of British subjects'. At least, that was the English version. Debate continues over the differences in meaning between the Maori and English versions of the Treaty.

Although many Europeans overlooked the Treaty, Maori cited it in countless petitions, legal actions, debates and appeals, all of which were largely ignored until the 1970s.

The text of the Maori and English versions of the Treaty can be seen at: www.govt.nz/aboutnz/treaty.php3.

The Waitangi Tribunal

The Waitangi Tribunal was established in 1975. Its role is to make recommendations on claims brought by Maori relating to the Treaty of Waitangi.

The Office of Treaty Settlements (www.ots.govt.nz) works with both the government and claimant groups to facilitate settlements on Treaty issues.

Final settlements since 21 September 1992

The following settlements are now complete and unconditional. Where legislation has been required it has been enacted. More claims are still being worked through.

Claimant group	Year Settled	Value ($)
Fisheries	1992/93	170 000 000
Ngati Whakaue	1993/94	5 210 000
Ngati Rangiteaorere	1993/94	760 000
Hauai	1993/94	715 682
Tainui Raupatu	1994/95	170 000 000
Waimakuku	1995/96	375 000
Rotoma	1996/97	43 931
Te Maunga	1996/97	129 032
Ngai Tahu/Kai Tahu	1996/97	170 000 000
Ngati Turangitukua	1998/99	5 000 000
Pouakani	1999/00	2 650 000*
Te Uri o Hau	1999/00	15 600 000
Ngati Ruanui	2000/01	41 000 000
Ngati Tama	2001/02	14 500 000
Total Settlement Redress		**594 883 645**

*Includes $650,000 paid in advance of settlement in 1990.

The King Movement/Kingitanga

Kingitanga was a confederation of tribes established to protect Maori land ownership and institutions. The Maori Queen today continues the tradition of the movement.

Maori Kings and Queens (Te Wherowhero family) and dates of accession

Potatau Te Wherowhero	1858
Tukaroto Matutaera Potatau Te Wherowhero Tawhiao (Potatau II)	1860
Potatau Te Wherowhero Mahuta	1894
Potatau Te Wherowhero Te Rata	1912
Koroki Te Rata Mahuta Tawhiao Potatau Te Wherowhero	1933
Te Arikinui (Queen) Te Atairangikahu	1966

- In 1892 the first Kotahitanga Maori Parliament met. Like the Kingitanga, this was an attempt to present Maori land grievances more powerfully to the Pakeha authorities.

Religious melding

Many influential Maori leaders took inspiration from Christianity and Judaism in forming new religious/political movements. Examples are:

- The warrior Te Kooti, who was a keen reader of the Old Testament, and founder of the Ringatu faith.
- Tahupotiki Wiremu Ratana, founder of the Ratana movement, which, in the late 1920s, also became a major political movement.

Historic sites

The New Zealand Historic Places Trust Pouhere Taonga is a charitable trust established by an Act of Parliament in 1954, which seeks to protect historic sites. (See www.historic.org.nz)

Government

Constitution

New Zealand is an independent state: a monarchy with a parliamentary government. Queen Elizabeth II of the United Kingdom has the title Queen of New Zealand.

Although the constitution is a monarchy in form, it operates democratically because of a long tradition of parliamentary government and a network of constitutional principles.

New Zealand's constitutional history can be traced back to 1840 when, by the Treaty of Waitangi, the Maori people exchanged their sovereignty for the guarantees of the Treaty and New Zealand became a British colony.

In the July 2002 election voter turnout was approximately 78% of eligible voters. Although slightly lower than the previous election, this turnout is high compared to other OECD countries. Non-voters are more likely to be on lower incomes, younger people and Maori or Pacific people.

Sovereigns of New Zealand and year of accession to throne

Victoria	1837
Edward VII	1901
George V	1910
Edward VIII	1936 (abdicated after 325 days)
George VI	1936
Elizabeth II	1952

The Crown and the Governor-General

The Governor-General is the representative of the Sovereign in New Zealand. The Sovereign appoints the Governor-General on the Prime Minister's recommendation, normally for five years. The Governor-General's main constitutional function is to arrange for the leader of the majority party in Parliament to form a government.

Lieutenant-Governors, Governors and Governors-General of New Zealand

Dependency

Lieutenant-Governor

Captain William Hobson, RN	1840–1841

Crown Colony

Governor

Captain William Hobson, RN	1841–1842
Captain Robert Fitzroy, RN	1843–1845
Captain George Grey	1845–1847
Governor-in-Chief	
Sir George Grey, KCB	1848–1853

Self–Governing Colony

Governor of New Zealand

Sir George Grey, KCB	1853–1853
Colonel Thomas Gore Browne, CB	1855–1861
Sir George Grey, KCB	1861–1868
Sir George Ferguson Bowen, GCMG	1868–1873
The Rt. Hon. Sir James Fergusson, Bt.	1873–1874
Marquess of Normanby, GCB, GCMG, PC	1875–1879
Sir Hercules George Robert Robinson, GCMG	1879–1880
The Hon. Sir Arthur Hamilton Gordon, GCMG	1880–1882
Lt. General Sir William Francis Drummond Jervois, GCMG, CB	1883–1889

Earl of Onslow, GCMG	1889–1892
Earl of Glasgow, GCMG	1892–1897
Earl of Ranfurly, GCMG	1897–1904
Lord Plunket, GCMG, KCVO	1904–1910
Lord Islington, KCMG, DSO, PC	1910–1912
Earl of Liverpool, GCMG, MVO, PC	1912–1917

Governor-General of New Zealand

Earl of Liverpool, GCB, GCMG, GBE, MVO, PC	1917–1920
Viscount Jellicoe, GCB, OM, GCVO	1920–1924
General Sir Charles Fergusson, Bt., GCMG, KCB, DSO, MVO	1924–1930
Viscount Bledisloe, GCMG, KBE, PC	1930–1935
Viscount Galway, GCMG, DSO, OBE, PC	1935–1941
Marshal of the RAF Sir Cyril Louis Norton Newall, GCB, OM, GCMG, CBE, AM	1941–1946
Lt. General the Lord Freyberg, VC, GCMG, KCB, KBE, DSO	1946–1952
Lt. General the Lord Norrie, GCMG, GCVO, CB, DSO, MC	1952–1957
Viscount Cobham, GCMG, TD	1957–1962
Brigadier Sir Bernard Fergusson, GCMG, GCVO, DSO, OBE	1962–1967
Sir Arthur Espie Porritt, Bt., GCMG, GCVO, CBE	1967–1972
Sir (Edward) Denis Blundell, GCMG, GCVO, KBE, QSO	1972–1977
The Rt. Hon. Sir Keith Jacka Holyoake, KG, GCMG, CH, QSO	1977–1980
The Hon. Sir David Stuart Beattie, GCMG, GCVO, QSO, QC	1980–1985

The Most Reverend Sir Paul Alfred Reeves, GCMG, GCVO, QSO	1985–1990
Dame Catherine Anne Tizard, GCMG, GCVO, DBE, QSO	1990–1996
The Rt. Hon. Sir Michael Hardie Boys, GNZM, GCMG, QSO	1996–2001
The Hon. Dame Silvia Rose Cartwright, PCNZM, DBE	2001–

Central government

New Zealand central government has three different branches:

- The Legislature (Parliament).
- The Executive (also generally known as the Government).
- The Judiciary (Judges).

Power is divided between these branches to protect the basic constitutional principles of the country.

The Legislature (Parliament)

Parliament is New Zealand's supreme law-making body, although it does delegate some of these powers, for example to local government.

Parliament consists of the Governor-General, and the House of Representatives. This House has 120 elected Members of Parliament (MPs). These members can be elected for an area (electorate MPs), or as representatives of their party (list MPs).

Elections are normally held every three years. In 1996 the Mixed Member Proportional (MMP) election system was used for the first time.

Mixed Member Proportional

Under MMP, each voter gets two votes:

- The party vote is for the party the voter most wants to see in Parliament.

- The electorate vote is for the candidate the voter wants as the local electorate MP.

To qualify for seats in Parliament, a party must gain 5% of all the party votes, or one electorate MP. If a party qualifies, its share of all 120 seats in Parliament will be close to its share of all the party votes. Therefore, in general, the total number of MPs a party has depends on the total number of party votes it gets at the election.

- Every electorate has about the same number of people in it. Over time, some areas can grow while others shrink, and so the boundary lines need adjusting. Any adjustments are carried out by the Representation Commission after each five-yearly Census.
- The quotas for Electoral Districts after the 2001 Census under the Electoral Act 1993 are:
  North Island General Electoral Districts 54,288 ± 5%
  South Island General Electoral Districts 54,296 ± 5%
  Maori Electoral Districts 53,130 ± 5%

Types of seats in 1999 election

61 General electorate (16 South Island, 45 North Island)
6 Maori electorate
53 party list (representing the proportion of the party vote)

Types of seats in 2002 election

62 General electorate (16 South Island, 46 North Island)
7 Maori electorate
51 party list

Gender split 2002 election

34 female MPs
86 male MPs

Maori can choose after each Census whether they wish to be on the Maori electoral roll or the General electoral roll. The number of Maori electorate seats can rise or fall depending on the number of Maori who choose to be registered on the Maori electoral roll. A change in the number of Maori seats can also affect the number of General seats in the North Island and the number of list seats.

Party representation in 1999 and 2002 elections

Act	9	9
Alliance	10	0
Green	7	9
Jim Anderton's Progressive Coalition	–	2
Labour	49	52
National	39	27
New Zealand First	5	13
United Future	1	8

- The New Zealand Bill of Rights Act 1990 exists to 'affirm, protect, and promote human rights and fundamental freedoms in New Zealand' as well as to 'affirm New Zealand's commitment to the International Covenant on Civil and Political Rights'.
- All Acts of Parliament can be found on: www.knowledge-basket.co.nz/gpprint

The Executive

After a general election, the Governor-General invites the leader of the party or parties with the most votes to become the Prime Minister, and to form a government. The new Prime Minister then selects a number of MPs as Ministers.

Each Minister has responsibility for various areas of administration (e.g. Health, Justice, Finance or Labour). The government's work in these administrative areas is carried out by the state sector.

Premiers and Prime Ministers (parties and terms of office)

Premiers

Henry Sewell	7 May 1856–20 May 1856
William Fox	20 May 1856–2 Jun 1856 12 Jul 1861–6 Aug 1862 28 Jun 1869–10 Sept 1872 3 Mar 1873–8 Apr 1873
Edward Stafford	2 Jun 1856–12 Jul 1861 16 Oct 1865–28 Jun 1869 10 Sep 1872–11 Oct 1872
Alfred Domet	6 Aug 1862–30 Oct 1863
Frederic Whitaker	30 Oct 1863–24 Nov 1864 21 Apr 1882–25 Sep 1883
Frederic Weld	24 Nov 1864–16 Oct 1865
George Waterhouse	11 Oct 1872–3 Mar 1873
Sir Julius Vogel	8 Apr 1873–6 Jul 1875 15 Feb 1876–1 Sep 1876
Daniel Pollen	6 Jul 1875–15 Feb 1876 1 Sep 1876–13 Sep 1876
Sir Harry Atkinson	13 Sep 1876–13 Oct 1877 (ministry reconstructed) 25 Sep 1883–16 Aug 1884 28 Aug 1884–3 Sep 1884 8 Oct 1887–24 Jan 1891
Sir George Grey	13 Oct 1877–8 Oct 1879
John Hall	8 Oct 1879–21 Apr 1882

Sir Robert Stout		16 Aug 1884–28 Aug 1884 3 Sep 1884–8 Oct 1887
John Ballance	Liberal	24 Jan 1891–*d* 27 Apr 1893
Richard Seddon	Liberal	1 May 1893–*d* 10 Jun 1906

Prime Ministers

William Hall-Jones	Liberal	21 Jun 1906–6 Aug 1906
Sir Joseph Ward	Liberal United	6 Aug 1906–28 Mar 1912 10 Dec 1928–28 May 1930
Thomas Mackenzie	Liberal	28 Mar 1912–10 Jul 1912
William Massey	Reform National	10 Jul 1912–12 Aug 1915 12 Aug 1919–*d* 10 May 1925
Sir Francis Bell	Reform	14 May 1925–30 May 1925
Joseph Coates	Reform	30 May 1925–10 Dec 1928
George Forbes	United Coalition	28 May 1930–22 Sep 1931 22 Sep 1931–6 Dec 1935
Michael Savage	Labour	6 Dec 1935–*d* 27 Mar 1940
Peter Fraser	Labour	1 Apr 1940–13 Dec 1949
Sidney Holland	National	13 Dec 1949–20 Sep 1857
Sir Keith Holyoake	National	20 Sep 1957–12 Dec 1957 12 Dec 1960–7 Feb 1972
Walter Nash	Labour	12 Dec 1957–12 Dec 1960
John Marshall (later Sir)	National	7 Feb 1972–8 Dec 1972
Norman Kirk	Labour	8 Dec 1973–*d* 31 Aug 1974
Wallace Rowling (later Sir)	Labour	6 Sep 1974–12 Dec 1975
Sir Robert Muldoon	National	12 Dec 1975–26 Jul 1984
David Lange	Labour	26 Jul 1984–8 Aug 1989

Geoffrey Palmer (later Sir)	Labour	8 Aug 1989–4 Sep 1990
Michael Moore	Labour	4 Sep 1990–2 Nov 1990
James Bolger	National	2 Nov 1990–12 Oct 1996
	Nat-NZ First Coal.	12 Oct 1996–8 Dec 1997
Jennifer Shipley	Nat-NZ First Coal.	8 Dec 1997–14 Aug 1998
	Nat Minority	31 Aug 1998–10 Dec 1999
Helen Clark	Lab-Alliance Coal.	10 Dec 1999–27 July 2002
	Lab Minority Coal.	27 July 2002–

Cabinet and the Executive Council

All Ministers become members of the Executive Council. Some are also invited to become part of the Cabinet. The Cabinet is the central decision-making and policy-making body of executive government, and coordinates the work of Ministers and Cabinet committees which examine issues in detail.

The Executive Council is a formal body with formal functions. It tenders advice to the Governor-General on the basis of policy formulated in Cabinet; it is the main vehicle for law-making by the executive.

For a list of current Ministers, the Cabinet and further information, see:
www.govt.nz and www.dpmc.govt.nz.

The state sector

The state sector includes the New Zealand Public Service, which is made up of 38 government departments, plus Crown entities and State-owned Enterprises (SOEs).

For a list of government departments, Crown entities and SOEs and their roles, see the Government Agencies list on www.govt.nz.

Government income and expenditure 2002/03

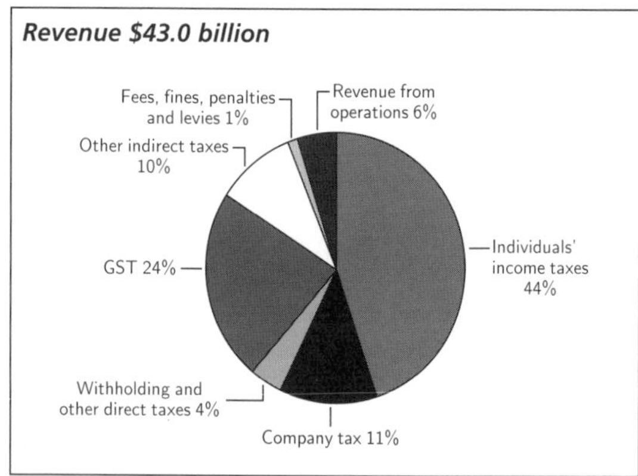

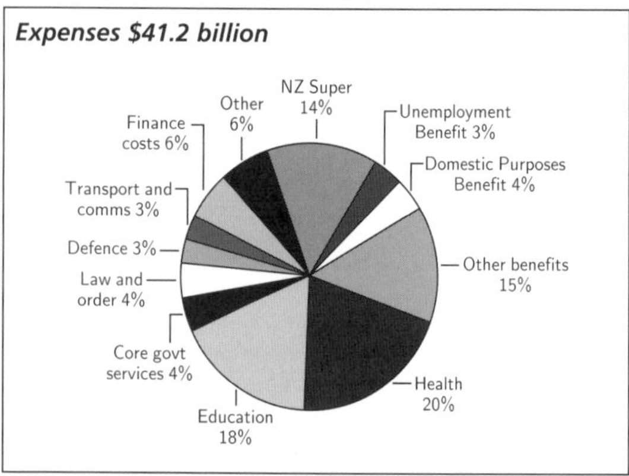

Source: Statistics New Zealand.

The Judiciary

Although Parliament makes the statute laws (Acts of Parliament), it is the job of the Judiciary to interpret and apply those statutes in court cases. These precedent-setting decisions then create what is called common law.

The independence of the Judiciary is an important principle of the New Zealand constitution.

Courts in New Zealand

There are 71 courts throughout New Zealand. They are:

- The Court of Appeal (the highest court, based in Wellington, hears and decides appeals from the High Court and appeals after jury trials in the District Court).
- High Courts (these hear and decide the most serious criminal charges, as well as large or important civil cases, some matrimonial property cases and some appeals from the District Court. They also oversee the power of the tribunals.)
- District Courts (these include Disputes Tribunals, Family Courts and the Youth Court).

New Zealanders also have access to the Privy Council in England, which can review special civil and criminal cases on appeal from the Court of Appeal. There is now some debate about the relevance of the Privy Council to the modern New Zealand legal system.

Tribunals

A number of specialised courts, tribunals, committees and boards act either as licensing or reviewing bodies or as dispute and appeal authorities. They monitor, regulate and enforce certain legislation. Examples are the Environment Court and the Motor Vehicle Disputes Tribunal.

The Waitangi Tribunal is a special tribunal established to hear Treaty of Waitangi claims.

Women in power

- In 2002, women filled all the important constitutional roles:
  - Governor General: The Hon. Dame Silvia Rose Cartwright, PCNZM, DBE.
  - Prime Minister: The Rt Hon Helen Clark.
  - Chief Justice: The Rt Hon Dame Sian Elias.
- In 1893, the same year that New Zealand women gained the vote, Elizabeth Yates was elected mayor of the Onehunga Borough Council.
- New Zealand's first woman MP was Elizabeth McCombs in 1933, for Lyttelton. (Women were eligible for Parliament in 1919.)
- Mabel Howard was the first Cabinet Minister, in 1947.
- 74 women have served in Parliament since 1933.
- The Lyttelton electorate has had the most women MPs (five).
- There were 35 women in the 2002 (46th) Parliament, of a total of 120 MPs.

Referendum issues

Until recently, there were few referenda to decide major political discussions in New Zealand, except those concerning alcohol. That has changed recently, although the outcomes of the referenda are not now binding on the legislators.

Citizen's initiated referenda (CIR)

For a CIR to take place, the petition must include the signatures of at least 10% of the total number of enrolled electors (as at the date the CIR is presented). If the petition has the required number of valid signatures, the government has to conduct a referendum within one year of the petition being submitted to Parliament.

Referendum issues and results

Issue	Result
Liquor licensing	Every election since 1911, except 1931 and 1951. In 1999 the last three 'dry' areas voted for liquor licensing so no longer a voting issue.
Off-course betting facilities	March, 1949, in favour
Extending bar hours from 6 to 10 pm	March, 1949, against
Compulsory military training	April, 1949, in favour
Changing political term from 3 to 4 years	Sept, 1967, against
End of 6 pm closing in bars and clubs	Sept, 1967, in favour
Change to proportional representation*	1992, in favour
Citizens Initiated Referenda Act**	1993 Act passed
Fire fighter numbers should not be cut	1995, in favour
Compulsory retirement savings scheme (government-initiated)	1997, against
House of Representative numbers to be cut	1999, in favour
Reform of the justice system	1999, in favour

* From First Past the Post (FPP) voting for MPs to Mixed Member Proportional (MMP).

** This ensures a non-binding referendum must be carried out if any citizen gathers the signatures of at least 10% of eligible voters.

New Zealand's rank in Corruption Perceptions Index (2001: 1 = least)

1. Finland
2. Denmark
3. New Zealand
4.} Iceland
4.} Singapore
6. Sweden
7. Canada
8. Netherlands
9. Luxembourg
10. Norway

Local government

New Zealand has a local government system largely independent of the central executive government. However, various Acts of Parliament give local government all its powers.

Local government elections are held on the second Saturday in October every three years. The next election will be in October 2004.

There are three kinds of local authorities:

- The 12 regional councils.
- The 74 territorial authorities, made up of:
  - 15 city councils including Nelson City which is a unitary authority.
  - 58 district councils, including the Gisborne, Tasman, and Marlborough District Councils, which are unitary authorities.
  - The Chatham Islands Council.
  - 147 community boards which report to some of the territorial councils.
- Seven special authorities.

Regional councils

These are directly elected, set their own rates, and elect their own chairperson. Their main functions are:

- Resource management.
- Biosecurity.
- Catchment control.
- Harbour administration.
- Regional civil defence.
- Regional land transport.

Territorial councils

These are directly elected, set their own rates, and have a community-elected mayor. Their many functions include:

- Community well-being and development.
- Environmental health and safety (including building control, civil defence, and environmental health matters).
- Infrastructure (roading and transport, sewerage, water/stormwater).
- Recreation and culture.
- Resource management, including land use planning and development control.

(Unitary councils do the work of both regional and territorial councils.)

Community boards

These can be either partly elected and partly appointed, or all elected. Their primary role is to advocate for their community, which is usually a ward within a territorial authority.

Special authorities

There are now few of these remaining, following reorganisation of local authorities in 1989. Those remaining mainly include scenic and recreation boards.

> The provinces were all abolished as authorities in 1876. Their usefulness remains, however, as an excuse for 12 different holidays in 12 different parts of the country, honouring the various beginnings of their shortish lives.

Honours system

There are two regular honours lists: one at New Year and one on the New Zealand observance of the Queen's birthday (the first Monday in June). Special lists, such as for bravery, are drawn up as required.

The main elements of the New Zealand Royal Honours System are: the Order of New Zealand; the New Zealand Order of Merit; the Queen's Service Order.

The Order of New Zealand (ONZ)

The ONZ is New Zealand's highest indigenous honour, limited to 20 ordinary members at any one time. It was instituted on 6 February 1987 to recognise outstanding service to the Crown and people of New Zealand.

Ordinary Members (limited to 20, as of 21 December 2001)

Te Arikinui Dame Te Atairangikaahu, DBE	6 Feb 1987
Sonja Margaret Loveday Davies, JP	6 Feb 1987
Sir Edmund Percival Hillary, KG, KBE	6 Feb 1987
June Daphne, Lady Blundell, QSO	6 Feb 1988
Dame Miriam Patricia Dell, DBE, JP	6 Feb 1993
Miss Margaret May Mahy	6 Feb 1993
The Hon. (Mrs) Tini Whetu Marama Tirikatene-Sullivan	6 Feb 1993
Sir Roy Allan McKenzie, KBE	17 Jun 1995
Dame Kiri Janette Te Kanawa, DBE, AC	17 Jun 1995
Sir (Frederick) Miles Warren, KBE	17 Jun 1995
Sir James Muir Cameron Fletcher	2 Jun 1997
Dr Ivan Lichter	2 Jun 1997
The Right Hon. James Brendan Bolger	31 Dec 1997
Kenneth George Douglas	31 Dec 1998
Dr Clifford Hamilton Whiting	31 Dec 1998
The Right Hon. Michael Kenneth Moore	31 Dec 1999
His Eminence Cardinal Thomas Stafford Williams	5 Jun 2000

Honorary Member

Sir Shridath Surendranath Ramphal, OE, GCMG, OM (Jamaica), AC, QC (UK)	6 Feb 1990

Additional Members (on death the vacancy is not filled)
(Appointed to mark Her Majesty's visit to New Zealand and the 1990 Commemoration.)

Her Majesty Queen Elizabeth the Queen Mother (UK)	6 Feb 1990
The Hon. Michael John Duffy (Australia)	6 Feb 1990
Miss Nene Janet Paterson Clutha (Janet Frame), CBE	6 Feb 1990
Arthur Leslie Lydiard, OBE	6 Feb 1990
Dame (Reubina) Ann Ballin, DBE	3 Jun 2002
The Right Hon. Sir Robin Brunskill Cooke, KBE, PC	3 Jun 2002
Professor Sir (Ian) Hugh Kawharu	3 Jun 2002
Dame Catherine Anne Tizard, DBE, QSO	3 Jun 2002

The New Zealand Order of Merit

This Order of Chivalry was instituted by Royal Warrant, dated 30 May 1996, and is for those persons who have rendered meritorious service to the Crown and nation or who have become distinguished by their contributions and merits.

As from 10 April 2000 the titles of Sir and Dame were discontinued for those given this award.

Queen's Service Order (QSO) and Associated Queen's Service Medal (QSM)

The Order and Medal arose out of the 1974–75 review of the honours system and the desire for an honour to highlight voluntary service to the community and service through elected and appointed public office.

New Zealand Gallantry and Bravery Awards

There are two categories, each with four levels.

- **The Gallantry Awards:** Recognise acts of gallantry by New Zealand Defence Force personnel, and others during war

or peace-keeping operations. They are:
- The Victoria Cross for New Zealand (VC).
- The New Zealand Gallantry Star (NZGS).
- The New Zealand Gallantry Decoration (NZGD).
- The New Zealand Gallantry Medal (NZGM).

- **The Bravery Awards:** These are for civilians who save or attempt to save the life of another person, and in so doing put their own lives at risk. They are:
  - The New Zealand Cross (NZC).
  - The New Zealand Bravery Star (NZBS).
  - The New Zealand Bravery Decoration (NZBD).
  - The New Zealand Bravery Medal (NZBM).

- The Victoria Cross has been won by British servicmen in New Zealand during the New Zealand Wars, by New Zealanders serving in the South African War and the two world wars. There have been 23 New Zealand-born Victoria Cross recipients. A total of 52 people received the Victoria Cross who were associated with New Zealand, either through birth, death, or the New Zealand forces.
- Charles Upham (1908–94) was only the third man, and the only combatant officer, to win a bar to the Victoria Cross. He won the Victoria Cross for exceptional gallantry and leadership in Crete in 1941, and then the bar for his actions in the Western Desert in 1942. After capture by the Germans, he was the only New Zealander to be held in Colditz, the special camp for habitual escapers.
- Moananui-a-kiwi Ngarimu (Ngati Porou and Te Whanau-a-Apanui, 1918–43) of Ruatoria is the only Maori to have won the Victoria Cross, awarded posthumously for his actions at Tebaga Gap in Tunis in March 1943, which took his life.

National emblems

Parliament buildings

Parliament House has three different buildings in Lambton Quay in Wellington: the neo-Gothic General Assembly Library (late 19th century), the Legislation Chamber (1918) and the circular Beehive (1977). (See www.ps.parliament.govt.nz/building.htm for a description of these.)

New Zealand flag

The purpose of New Zealand's first flag of 1835 was to protect trading ships built in New Zealand. It had been chosen by representatives of Te Runanga Kohuiarau (the Confederation of the United Tribes of New Zealand). King William IV then directed the Admiralty to recognise and protect any ship bearing this flag.

The current New Zealand flag consists of two main elements, the Union flag of Great Britain and the four stars of the Southern Cross. It was adopted in 1902, mostly as a result of the patriotic fervour at the time of the South African war.

For more information on the flag see the Ministry of Culture and Heritage on www.mch.govt.nz/nzflag/history.htm.

New Zealand coat of arms

The coat of arms is confined to official purposes. New Zealand has had its own coat of arms since 1911, and it was last revised in 1956.

National anthems

New Zealand has two national anthems of equal status: 'God Defend New Zealand' and 'God Save The Queen'.

God Defend New Zealand

God of nations at thy feet
in the bonds of love we meet.
Hear our voices, we entreat,
God defend our free land.
Guard Pacific's triple star
From the shafts of strife and war,
Make her praises heard afar,
God defend New Zealand.

Men of every creed and race
Gather here before thy face,
Asking thee to bless this place,
God defend our free land.
From dissension, envy, hate,
And corruption guard our state,
Make our country good and great,
God defend New Zealand.

Peace, not war, shall be our boast,
But, should foes assail our coast,
Make us then a mighty host,
God defend our free land.
Lord of battles in thy might,
Put our enemies to flight,
Let our cause be just and right,
God defend New Zealand.

Aotearoa

E Ihoa Atua,
O nga Iwi! Matoura,
Ata whaka rongona;
Me aroha roa.
Kia hua ko te pai;
Kia tau to atawhai;
Manaakitia mai
Aotearoa.

Ona mano tangata
Kiri whereo, kiri ma,
Iwi Maori Pakeha
Repeke katoa,
Nei ka tono ko nga he
Mau e whakaahu ke,
Kia ora marire
Aotearoa.

Tona mana kia tu!
Tona kaha kia u;
Tona rongo hei paku
Ki te ao katoa
Aua rawa nga whawhai,
Nga tutu a tata mai;
Kia tupu nui ai
Aotearoa.

Let our love for thee increase,
May thy blessings never cease,
Give us plenty, give us peace,
God defend our free land.
From dishonour and from shame
Guard our country's spotless name,
Crown her with immortal fame,
God defend New Zealand.

May our mountains ever be
Freedom's ramparts on the sea,
Make us faithful unto thee,
God defend our free land.
Guide her in the nation's van,
Preaching love and truth to man,
Working out thy glorious plan.
God defend New Zealand.

Waiho tona takiwa
Ko te ao marama;
Kia whiti tona ra
Taiawhio noa.
Ko te hae me te ngangau
Meinga kia kore kau;
Waiho i te rongo mau
Aotearoa.

Tona pai me toitu;
Tika rawa, pono pu;
Tona noho, tana tu;
Iwi no Ihoa.
Kaua mona whakama;
Kia hau te ingoa;
Kia tu hei tauira;
Aotearoa.

- At official occasions, normally only the first verse of 'God Defend New Zealand' is sung.
- New Zealand officially had only one national anthem, 'God Save the Queen', until 1977 when Thomas Bracken's 'God Defend New Zealand' was given equal staus. Bracken wrote the lyrics as a poem in the early 1870s, and offered a prize for the best musical setting, won by John Woods, an Otago school teacher. The song was declared the country's 'National Hymn' in 1940.

International relations

The Ministry of Foreign Affairs and Trade (MFAT), Te Manatu Aorere, is responsible for advising and assisting the New Zealand government in its relations with other countries.

New Zealand diplomatic posts

New Zealand has 47 diplomatic and consular posts located in 41 countries and 46 honorary consulates. Multiple accreditation allows New Zealand representatives to cover 76 other countries from their bases (e.g. the New Zealand ambassador to Mexico is cross-credited to Venezuela and Guatemala).

Diplomatic representatives to New Zealand

There are currently 37 embassies and high commissions in Wellington with another 63 accredited to New Zealand but located in other countries (mostly Canberra, Australia). This brings the number of foreign representatives to 100.

Some international organisations to which New Zealand belongs

- Asian Development Bank: New Zealand has shares in this bank for financing 33 Asia-Pacific developing countries.
- Asia Pacific Economic Cooperation (APEC) forum: New Zealand hosted the APEC summit in 1999, the smallest nation to do so at that time. (See www.apecsec.org.sg for details of APEC work.)
- Commonwealth: Includes 54 countries representing 1.7 billion people. New Zealand is a founding member since its entry in 1931.
- International Labour Organisation (ILO): Has 174 member countries and administers 180 conventions (legally binding international labour standards).
- Organisation for Economic Cooperation and Development (OECD): This is an important forum for the

governments of the industrialised democracies. New Zealand is particularly interested in contributing to its agricultural policies.

- Pacific Island Forum: Was the South Pacific Forum, now made up of 16 Pacific nations.
- United Nations (UN): New Zealand was a founding member in 1945, and is a member of all its major specialised agencies.
- World Bank: New Zealand contributes to the International Development Association (IDA) of the World Bank's funds.
- World Trade Organisation (WTO): Former New Zealand Prime Minister Mike Moore was appointed Director-General of the WTO from 1999 to 2002.

Sample environmental organisations to which New Zealand belongs

Commission for Sustainable Development
The Global Environment Facility
The South Pacific Regional Environment Programme
The International Whaling Commission

New Zealand has a close relationship as a 'dialogue partner' with the Association of South-East Asian Nations (ASEAN). ASEAN countries are very important to New Zealand in terms of trade; for example, many ASEAN students and tourists come here.

Development aid

New Zealand's development aid is concentrated on Pacific Island states and the poorer East and South-East Asian countries. Support is also given to selected countries in southern Africa and Latin America and to a range of multilateral and regional institutions.

New Zealand's Official Development Assistance (NZODA) Programme is funded by payments set by Parliament and administered by the New Zealand Agency for International Development (NZAID). (See www.nzaid.govt.nz)

Net official development assistance programme 2002/03

Bilateral aid	**$(000)**
Pacific	80 758
Asia	34 795
Africa	4 770
Americas	5 300
Education and training	20 320
Voluntary agencies	19 060
Other bilateral	2 750
Multilateral aid	**$(000)**
Commonwealth agencies	4 034
Pacific agencies	12 820
Int. financial institutions	26 167
United Nations agencies	15 395
Other multilateral	4 225
NZ aid total	**230 394**

Some comparisons of net official development assistance as a percentage of Gross National Product, 1998 and 2000:

	1998	2000
Australia	0.27%	0.27%
Ireland	0.30%	0.30%
Sweden	0.72%	0.80%
New Zealand	0.27%	0.25%
United States	0.10%	0.10%

New Zealand territories

Tokelau

Tokelau consists of three small atolls in the South Pacific with a combined land area of 12 sq km, and a population of around 1500. It is a non-self-governing territory.

Each of the Tokelauan atolls consists of a number of low-lying islets enclosing a lagoon, and the greatest height above sea level is just 5 m. The territory is at risk from the projected rise in sea levels due to 'global warming'.

Ross Dependency

The Ross Dependency consists of the land, ice-shelf and islands of Antarctica between longitude 160° east to 150° west, and south of latitude 60° south. The area was proclaimed as a British settlement in 1923, although the 1959 Antarctic Treaty did not confirm this. New Zealand operates Scott Base there on a permanent basis for scientists.

New Zealand is an original party to the Antarctic Treaty, which requires the Antarctic to be used for peaceful and scientific purposes only.

- New Zealand has always been closely associated with Antarctica, with New Zealander Alexander von Tunzelmann probably the first person to set foot on the continent, at Cape Adare, on 24 January 1895. New Zealanders have also been involved in the major exploratory expeditions of Antarctica.
- The Cook Islands became a self-governing territory in free association with New Zealand in 1974, and Niue did the same in 1974. Cook Islanders, Niueans and Tokelauans are New Zealand citizens.

Defence

The New Zealand Defence Force is made up of the Royal New Zealand Naval Forces, the New Zealand Army and the Royal New Zealand Air Force, along with civilian employees.

International defence relationships

- Australia is New Zealand's closest ally. This was acknowledged in the 1991 policy of Closer Defence Relations. New Zealanders and Australians have served alongside each other in numerous conflicts since the South African War.
- New Zealand has contributed to United Nations peace support operations since 1954.
- New Zealand also has a long history of involvement in non-UN peace support operations, such as the Multinational Force and Observers in the Sinai, to which we have contributed since 1982.
- The Five Power Defence Arrangements: in 1971 New Zealand, Australia and Great Britain agreed to come to the aid of Singapore and/or Malaysia if needed.
- Mutual Assistance Programme: New Zealand's commitment to regional security in most ASEAN and Pacific countries through military training, advice and cooperation; and using the engineering and trade skills of the New Zealand armed forces in development work.
- Australia New Zealand United States (ANZUS): The security treaty between these three nations was made in 1952. However, the ANZUS council has not met since 1984 as New Zealand refused access to US warships as part of its anti-nuclear stance. The US suspended security obligations to New Zealand on 11 August 1986.
- Other countries: defence representatives are attached to many of New Zealand's diplomatic missions, as do other countries with missions here or accredited here.

Examples of peace-keeping commitments

- UN Transitional Administration in East Timor.
- Peace Monitoring Group, Bougainville.
- International Peace Monitoring Team, Solomon Islands.
- UN Mission in Sierra Leone.
- Stabilisation Force, Bosnia and Herzegovina.
- UN Mission of Observers in Prevlaka, Croatia.
- UN Interim Administration Mission in Kosovo.
- Multinational Force and Observers, Sinai.
- UN Truce Supervision Organisation, Israel, Lebanon, Syria and Egypt.
- International Security Assistance Force, Afghanistan.

The New Zealand defence forces also provide humanitarian assistance, which can be in various forms, from engineering to medical assistance. The most common UN humanitarian operations in which New Zealand has been involved are demining. New Zealand demining operations are currently being carried out in Laos, Cambodia and Mozambique.

Major war casualties (killed and wounded)

South Africa (1899–1902)	228	166
First World War (1914–18)	16 697	41 262
Second World War (1939–45)	11 625	17 000
Korea (1950–57)	41	81
Malaya/Malaysia (1948–31, 1960, 1963–66)	26	30
Vietnam (1964–72)	37	187

Defence expenditure

Defence spending (Vote Defence and Vote Defence Force) is voted by Parliament to the New Zealand Defence Force and the Ministry of Defence. The budgeted defence spending for

2002/03 was $1.8 billion. This amounts to 3% of total government expenditure.

The long-term development plan for the New Zealand Defence Force envisages a $3 billion spending programme on Defence equipment over 10 years.

Number of defence personnel (June 2002)

Navy	2 294
Army	6 612
Air Force	2 261
Civilians (incl. MOD & NZDF)	1 841
Total	**13 008**

Comparison of defence expenditure (% of GDP) 1995 and 1998

Australia	2.2	1.9
Canada	1.6	1.2
New Zealand	1.4	1.4
Sweden	2.6	2.3
United Kingdom	3.4	2.7
United States	3.9	3.0

Anzac Day

On 25 April 1915, Australian and New Zealand forces landed on Gallipoli peninsula, hoping to defeat the Turks there. Of the 8556 New Zealanders who served in this unsuccessful campaign, 2515 were killed in action, 206 died of diseases and other causes and 4752 were wounded. The date of that landing has become our national day of remembrance for all New Zealanders who have given their lives in war.

Population

All information in this section is taken from Statistics New Zealand (www.stats.govt.nz) and *The New Zealand Official Yearbook 2002.*

Census figures

The Census is the official count of population and dwellings in New Zealand. The questions asked also provide a snapshot of our society at a point in time. The most recent Census was on 6 March 2001.

On the 2001 Census night 3,737,277 people were counted as usually living in this country and 83,472 were visitors, making a total of 3,820,749.

Census facts

- The census of usually resident population of New Zealand in 2001 showed an increase of 118,975 or 3.3% since the 1996 Census. This is less than half that experienced between 1991 and 1996 (7.2%).
- There was a net outward migration flow of 8000 between 1996 and 2001, compared with a net inward migration flow of 78,000 between 1991 to 1996.
- The largest usually resident population count was Auckland region (not city) with 1,158,891 or 31% of the national population.
- The fastest growing region was Tasman, in the South Island, where the usually resident population increased by 8.9% or 3381 to 41,352.
- The fastest growing territorial authority was also in the South Island: Queenstown-Lakes with a 19.3% or 2757 increase to 17,040 in usually resident population count since the 1996 Census.

Total population, 1858–2001 Censuses

1858	115 462
1874	344 984
1878	458 007
1881	534 030
1886	620 451
1891	668 651
1896	743 214
1901	815 862
1906	936 309
1911	**1 058 312**
1916	1 149 225
1921	1 271 668
1926	1 408 139
1936	1 573 812
1945	1 702 330
1951	1 939 472
1956	**2 174 062**
1961	2 414 984
1966	2 676 919
1971	2 862 631
1976	**3 129 383**
1981	3 143 307
1986	3 263 284
1991	3 373 927
1996	3 618 302
2001	3 737 277

Notes: The census years 1861, 1864, 1876 and 1871 omitted as no Maori census taken those years. 1991 onwards records resident population, not 'de facto' as previously.

Population definitions

- 'De facto' population measures excluded New Zealanders temporarily overseas but included temporary visitors. This was the measure used until 1991.
- 'Usually resident' population measures made adjustments for the estimated net undercounts (people not filling in Census forms) and for New Zealand residents temporarily overseas. This measure has been used since 1991.

The least increase in the New Zealand population was between the 1976 and 1981 Censuses, where the population increased only 40,042 or 1.29%.

Population clock

New Zealand's population is estimated to increase by one person every eight minutes and 52 seconds. This is based on the estimated resident population at 30 September 2001 and the following component settings:

- One birth every nine minutes and 24 seconds.
- One death every 19 minutes and 57 seconds.
- A net migration gain of one New Zealand resident every 17 minutes and 40 seconds.

At the end of June 2002 New Zealand's resident population was provisionally estimated at 3.94 million, of which half of the population were over 34.9 years old, and 12% of the population were aged 65 years and over.

North and South Islands population

Between 1996 and 2001 the population usually resident in the North Island increased by 111,627 or 4.1% to 2,829,798. That is 75.7% of the total population.

The South Island resident population increased by 7368 or 0.8% to 906,753. That is 24.3% of the total population.

The region that experienced the biggest decline in population between 1996 and 2001 was the West Coast, where the population fell 6.8% (2211) to 30,303.

Urbanisation comparisons (selected countries and continents)

Country/Continent (total pop., million)	Urban proportion of total pop. (%)	Largest city, 1995 (million)
Singapore (3.4)	100	Singapore (3.3)
United Kingdom (58)	89	London (7.6)
New Zealand (3.6)	**85**	**Auckland (1)**
Australia (18)	85	Sydney (3.6)
Japan (125)	78	Tokyo (27)
United States (269)	76	New York (16.3)
World (5768)	***46***	
China (1,232)	31	Shanghai (13.6)
India (944)	27	Bombay (15.1)

The territorial authority with the smallest population count on Census night 2001 was the Chatham Islands District with 720 people.

The Quality of Life Project (www.bigcities.govt.nz) is an ongoing study of the quality of life in New Zealand's big cities.

The 2001 Census usually resident population count of the major cities in descending order is:

Auckland	367 734
Christchurch	316 227
Manukau	283 200
North Shore	184 821
Waitakere	168 750
Wellington	163 824
Hamilton	114 921
Dunedin	114 342
Lower Hutt	95 478

Components of population change

Population change has two main components:

- Natural increase (births over deaths).
- Net migration (the difference between arrivals and departures).

For the year ending 30 June 2002 the population grew an estimated 58,300 or 1.5%. This was due to a natural increase of 25,500 and a net permanent and long-term migration inwards of 32,820.

Natural increase: births and deaths (March 2002)

- 54,700 live births were registered in New Zealand, down 3% on the previous year.
- Latest birth rates suggest that New Zealand women average 1.97 births per woman.
- The 30 to 34 year age group had the highest fertility rate (113 per 1000) during the March 2002 year.
- The average age of women having children was 29.5 years.

- There were 28,100 deaths registered during the March 2002 year.
- Births exceeded deaths (called the natural increase of population) by 26,600.

Booming and blooming: over 1.1 million New Zealanders were born between 1946 and 1965. The most babies were born in 1961, when half of all women were married before they were 22, and 65,390 babies were born.

Implied family size (births per 1000 pop and total fertility rate)*

1921	23.24	–
1941	24.02	2.93
1961	26.95	4.31
1981	16.09	2.01
2001	14.47	2.01

*This is the average number of births a woman would have during her reproductive life.

- The current New Zealand birth rate is about 4% below the level (2.10 births per woman) required for the population to replace itself, without migration.
- However, New Zealand's fertility rate is one of the highest among the OECD countries. It is at least 10% higher than the fertility rate for countries such as:
  Australia (1.7 births per woman)
  Canada (1.6)
  England and Wales (1.7)
  France (1.8)
  Sweden (1.5).

Life expectancy at birth, 1880–2001

Period Born	Male	Female
1880–92	54.4	57.3
1921–22	62.8	65.4
1960–62	68.4	73.8
1998	76.0	81.0

New Zealanders' life expectancy increased by 3.2 years from 1988–98, the highest increase of all the OECD countries.

Net migration

People who wish to immigrate to New Zealand to live are assessed under one of five main categories: General Skills (often called the 'points system'), Investor, Entrepreneur, Family and Humanitarian.

There is also a quota system for Samoans (up to 1100 per year) wishing to move to New Zealand, and a refugee quota (usually 750 people per year).

Net long-term migration (gain or loss)

1992	3 590
1998	450
1999	–11 370
2000	–9 760
2001	–9 270
2002	32 820

Note: Long-term departures include New Zealand residents departing for an intended period of 12 months or more (or permanently), plus overseas visitors departing from New Zealand after a stay of 12 months or more.

Half of the people in New Zealand on Census night 2001 had changed their usual address at least once since 1996. People in the 25 to 29 year age range are particularly mobile, with seven out of 10 having changed their usual address since 1996.

Permanent and long-term migration

Permanent or long-term arrivals exceeded departures by just over 32,800 for the year ended June 2002. This was the highest recorded net inflow for any year. It reverses the trend from the 1996 to 2001 Censuses.

- There were 92,700 arrivals, up 23,200 (or 33%) on the year ended June 2001.
- There were 59,900 departures, down 18,900 (or 24%) on the year ended June 2001.

Permanent and long-term arrivals were:

- New Zealand citizens: 25,000
- Non-New Zealand citizens 67,700; major groups were:
  - China (13,800)
  - India (5800)
  - The United Kingdom (4900)
  - South Africa (3200)
  - Fiji (2400)
  - Japan (2300)

Permanent and long-term departures were:

- New Zealand citizens: 44,900 (down 18,400 on the year ended June 2001).
- Non-New Zealand citizens: 15,000 (down 500 on the year ended June 2001).

The overall result was that in the year ended June 2002 there was a net permanent and long-term outflow of 19,900 New Zealand citizens, and a net permanent and long term inflow of 52,700 non-New Zealand citizens.

In the year ended June 2002, there was a net outflow to Australia of 13,700, less than half the net outflow of 31,000 in the June 2001 year.

Ethnicity

The 2001 Census showed New Zealand is a country of increasing ethnic diversity. Ethnic affiliations include:

- **European:** declined from 83% of the total in the 1991 Census to 80% in 2001.
- **Maori:** one in seven people (526,281) were counted in the Maori ethnic group, an increase of 21% since 1991. Most Maori continue to live in the northern regions. Nearly 90% live in the North Island and nearly 60% live in Northland, Auckland, Waikato and the Bay of Plenty. Nearly nine out of 20 people in the Gisborne region are of Maori ethnicity. The number of Maori in the South Island has increased 38% since 1991 to 64,650.
- **Asian Peoples:** almost 240,000 or one in 15 people were of Asian ethnicity. Counts of people of Asian ethnicity have more than doubled between 1991 and 2001. Two-thirds of people of Asian ethnicity live in the Auckland region and one in eight live in the Wellington region.
- **Pacific Peoples:** Since the early 1960s there has been a steady inflow of people from the Pacific Islands. In 1981 this population was just over 100,000. In the 2001 Census, one in 16 or 231,801 people in New Zealand were of Pacific ethnicity. Half or 115,017 of those were Samoan, an increase of 34% since the 1991 Census. The next largest groups were Cook Island Maori (52,569), Tongan (40,716), Niuean (20,148), Fijian (7041), Tokelauan (6204), and Tuvalu Islander (1965). Two-thirds of those of Pacific Peoples ethnicity live in the Auckland region.

Fastest growing of top 50 ethnic groups

	2001 Count	Increase from 1991
Korean	19 026	1 946%
Arab	2 856	1 514%
Croat	2 502	1 363%
Iraqi	2 145	772%
South African	14 889	642%
Russian	3 084	543%

In the Auckland region, one in eight people are of Asian ethnicity, one in eight of Pacific peoples' ethnicity and one in 10 of Maori ethnicity.

People born overseas

Almost one in five New Zealand residents were born overseas compared with one in six in 1991 and one in three in 1901.

- In the Auckland region, one in three people were born overseas; one in nine were born in Asia.
- Almost three-quarters of people born in the Pacific Islands and two-thirds of those born in Asia live in Auckland.
- Almost one in four people in the Wellington region were born overseas, while fewer than one in 15 people in the Southland region were born overseas.
- The main countries of overseas birthplace were:

England	178 203	China	38 949
Australia	56 259	Scotland	28 680
Samoa	47 118		

- While the number of New Zealand residents born in Europe has shown a small decline since 1996, there have been large increases from Africa, the Middle East and Asia.

Greatest increase in counts of overseas birthplace

	Absolute increase from 1996	Increase from 1996
China	19 431	100%
South Africa	14 727	130%
India	8 082	63%
Fiji	6 951	37%
Korea	5 751	47%

An ageing population

- The median age of the population has increased from 31 years at the 1991 Census to 35 years in 2001.
- In the 1901 Census the median age was 22 years.
- 450,426 or nearly one in eight people are aged 65 years and over compared with one in 25 in 1901.
- The Marlborough region has the highest proportion aged 65 years and over with nearly one in six.
- The Auckland region has the lowest proportion aged 65 years and over with one in 10.
- The Gisborne region has the highest proportion of those aged under 15 years with more than one in four.
- There was an increase of 26% in the number of people aged 85 years and over between 1996 and 2001.

- Almost half a million people were aged 65 years and over at the time of the 2001 Census. The number of people aged 65 years and over has more than doubled since 1951, increasing from 177,500 to 450,400.
- Over the last 100 years the Maori population has been concentrated in the younger age groups, a result of consistently high fertility.

Social framework

Summary and OECD comparisons of social connectedness

- Unpaid work outside the home:
  - 59% of the population aged 12 and over spent some time during the last four weeks doing unpaid work outside the home (1999).
  - Women and Maori are more likely to undertake unpaid work outside the home.
- Telephone and Internet access in the home (Census 2001):
  - The higher the household income, the greater the level of Internet and telecommunication access.
  - 72% of all New Zealanders (end 2001) have access to the Internet.
  - Just over one in four households have access to a fax.
  - Over 96% of households have access to a telephone.
  - One in 25 households do not have telephone, fax or Internet access.
  - Internet access is less likely among Maori and Pacific families, families with unemployed adults and sole parent families.
  - Above average for Internet access in OECD.
- Participation in family/whanau activities and regular contact with family/friends:
  - 71% of adults had family or friends over for dinner at least once a month in the previous year and 87% engage in family/whanau activities (2000).
  - Older people and Europeans/Pakeha are less likely to be involved in family activities.
- Membership of and involvement in groups:
  - 70% of adults belonged to community organisations or groups (1999).

- Non-Maori are less likely to belong to sports clubs and cultural organisations. Women are more likely to belong to church groups, hobby groups and community service organisations. Men more likely to belong to sports clubs and unions.

Usual household composition, 1991 and 2001 Censuses

One family only (with/without others)	841 944	909 084
Two or more families (with/without others)	19 818	28 440
Other multi-person household	68 820	70 434
One-person households	235 986	307 635

Although New Zealand has traditionally had a high rate of home ownership, this rate has declined between 1991 and 2001.

- In 1991, 73.8% of households owned their dwellings with or without a mortgage.
- In 2001, approximately two-thirds of households (868,656 or 67.8%) owned their dwellings. Those aged over 65 are most likely to reside in owner-occupied dwellings.

The number of motor vehicles owned by New Zealand households has increased steadily over the last three censuses. Eighty-nine per cent or 1,158,459 households had access to at least one motor vehicle in the 2001 Census.

Marriages/divorces and de facto relationships

These are the major trends in marriage, divorce and de facto relationships as of December 2001.

- **Fewer marriages:** the marriage rate per 1000 not-married population aged 16 years and over dropped from 15.6 in 2000 to 14.8 marriages per 1000 in 2001.

Marriages	
1999	21 085
2000	20 655
2001	20 000

- **Later marriages:** the median ages for men and women marrying for the first time in 2001 was 29.3 and 27.5 years respectively. This is about six years older than in the early 1970s.
- **Stable divorce rate:** the divorce rate (number of marriage dissolutions per 1000 existing marriages) decreased from 12.6 in 1999 to 12.3 in 2000, and remained stable at 12.3 divorces in 2001.
  - There were 9700 divorces in 2001.
  - The median age at divorce was 41.9 years for men and 39.3 years for women.
- **More remarriages:** the proportion of marriages that involve the remarriage of one or both partners has grown. In 1971, one in six marriages involved the remarriage of one or both partners. In 2001 this proportion grew to just over one in three of all legal marriages.
- **De facto unions are more common:** in 1996, about one in four men and women aged 15 to 44 years who were in partnerships were not legally married. By 2001, this figure had increased to around three in 10. For men and women under 25 years of age, those living in a de facto relationship outnumbered those legally married.

Divorce and children

Just under half of all marriages dissolved in 2001 involved children (under 18 years). Of those divorces involving children, there was an average number of 1.9 children per divorce. Just under half of those children were under 10 years of age in 2001.

Teenagers comprised 32% of all females who married in 1971, but only 3% in 2001. Among partnered women aged 15 to 19 years, nine out of 10 were living in a de facto union at the time of the 2001 Census.

Length of marriages

A significant proportion of marriages last a relatively short time. Divorces are most common among those couples who have been married for five to nine years. They accounted for one-quarter of all divorces in 2000.

The most marriages in any one year was in 1971 when 27,199 weddings took place. This was a marriage rate of 45.5 marriages per 1000 not-married population aged 16 years and over.

Median age of childbearing

	Nuptial	Ex-nuptial	Total
1962	26.5	22.1	26.2
1965	25.9	21.2	25.5
1970	25.4	20.8	24.9
1975	25.6	20.5	25.0
1980	26.5	21.2	25.7
1985	27.5	22.4	26.6
1990	29.0	23.6	27.7
1995	30.4	24.7	28.6
2000	31.3	26.1	29.7
2001	31.4	26.1	29.8

Notes: 1. Figures are for a pregnancy resulting in either live or stillborn children, and each birth event is counted only once, regardless of whether a single or multiple birth results. 2. Figures from 1991 onwards are based on the resident population, not the de facto as previously.

Number of births

	Nuptial	Ex-nuptial	Total
1962	59 787	5 227	65 014
1965	53 516	6 531	60 047
1970	53 774	8 276	62 050
1975	47 232	9 407	56 639
1980	39 685	10 857	50 542
1985	38 877	12 921	51 798
1990	39 674	20 479	60 153
1995	34 187	23 484	57 671
2000	32 142	24 463	56 605

Important family legislation

- **Guardianship Act 1968:** defines the authority of parents as guardians of their children and the powers of the court in relation to children.
- **Matrimonial Property Act 1976:** provides for the just distribution of property upon divorce.
- **Family Proceedings Act 1980:** the only grounds for divorce is that a marriage has broken down irreconcilably. The parties must have lived apart for two years to prove this.
- **Child Support Act 1992:** defines a regime for assessing non-custodial parental support of children.
- **Domestic Violence Act 1995:** provides protection for the victims of domestic violence.
- **Property (Relationships) Act 1976:** is the new title for the Matrimonial Property Act. From February 2002 it applies to de facto heterosexual couples and same sex couples, as well as married couples.

Religions

Sample main religious affiliations (1991 and 2001 Censuses)

Christian		
Anglican	732 048	584 793
Catholic	498 612	486 012
Presbyterian	553 386	431 547
Methodist	139 494	120 705
Baptist	70 155	51 426
Latter Day Saints/Mormon	48 009	39 912
Pentecostal	49 596	67 239
Brethren	21 915	20 406
Salvation Army	19 992	12 618
Jehovah's Witness	19 182	17 826
Seventh Day Adventist	15 675	14 868
Maori Christian		
Ratana	47 595	48 975
Ringatu	8 049	15 288
Others		
Hindu	18 036	39 864
Buddhist	12 762	41 634
Islam/Moslem	6 096	23 631
Spiritualism & New Age rel.	5 196	16 062
Judaism	3 126	6 636
No religion	670 455	1 028 052
Object to answering	251 709	239 244

Religions facts

- Some 17% of people are Anglicans, 14% Catholics and the Presbyterian group 11%.
- The number of Catholics increased by 12,900 between 1996 and 2001, while the number of Anglicans (-46,971) along with the Presbyterian group (-38,895) decreased.
- The count of Anglicans exceeded that of the other denominations in all regions except Auckland (where Catholics were largest) and Otago and Southland (where the Presbyterian group was the largest).
- The main denominations in the 1901 Census were Church of England (41%), Presbyterian (23%), Catholic (14%), and Methodist (11%).
- In the 1901 Census only one in 30 people did not give a religious affiliation. Almost four out of 10 people did not specify an affiliation in the 2001 Census.

Largest increase in religions (1996–2001)

Islam	74%
Spiritualism	64%
Hindu	56%
Buddhist	48%

Languages

English and Maori are the official languages of New Zealand. Maori became an official language and legally protected taonga or 'treasure' under the Maori Language Act 1987.

Data from the 2001 Census showed that:

- English is the predominant language spoken.
- The number of multilingual people increased by 20% from the 1996 Census to 562,113 or nearly one in six.
- Excluding children under five years of age, one in 50 do not speak English.
- The languages most widely spoken after English were:

Maori	160 527
Samoan	81 036
French	49 722
Yue (Cantonese)	37 143
German	33 981

English speakers

New Zealand English shares many common traits with Australian (including the denial of this observation). Much of the slang comes from historical similarities.

New Zealand English is characterised by the high number of Maori words, either borrowed directly, as in the names of plants and animals, or easily understood such as 'moana' for sea. In other cases the Maori often takes precedence, for example, 'whanau' for 'extended family' and 'mana' for 'prestige' or 'status'.

Sample Kiwi slang expressions

Greasies: fish and chips
Long drop: outside toilet (unflushing variety)
Ratbag: rogue
Smoko: morning or afternoon tea break

Maori speakers

- One in four (130,482) people of Maori ethnicity speak the Maori language.
- Nearly half of Maori language speakers are aged under 25 years.
- Over one in three people of Maori ethnicity in the Gisborne region speak the Maori language, with just under one in three in Bay of Plenty and Northland.

Sample Maori proverbs

- Ka hinga te totara o te wao nui a Tane: The falling of the totara tree in the great forest of Tane. (*Said upon the death of a chief or great man.*)
- He manga wai koia kia kore e whitikia: It is a big river indeed that cannot be crossed (*Make light of difficulties and they will disappear.*)
- He taru tawhiti: A thing from afar (i.e. disease.) (*A modern saying, referring to the many diseases brought by Europeans.*)
- He waha huka: A frothy mouth. (*Applied to one who makes empty promises – during the Second World War Sir Apirana Ngata composed a song called Hitara Waha Huka, Hitler the frothy mouthed.*)

- Over 700 Te Kohanga Reo pre-school centres (the first opened in 1982) provide Maori language total immersion education for over 13,000 children.
- Kohanga reo centres are subsidised by government and provide an important base in bilingualism for Maori along with cultural education.

Social welfare

Major social welfare legislation

1898	Means-tested old age pension
1911	Widows' pension
1926	Family allowances
1930	Limited unemployment relief
1936	Invalids', deserted wives' benefits
1938	Social Security Act
1946	Universal family benefit (abolished 1991)
1973	Domestic purposes benefit
1975	Disability allowance
1977	National superannuation scheme

Social Security Act 1938

The Social Security Act 1938 was pioneering legislation. It established:

- Payment according to means by general taxation, withdrawals according to needs.
- Universal superannuation regardless of income.
- Universal national health system.
- New classes of benefits, such as orphans', sickness and emergency benefits.
- All benefits to be brought under one system.
- Less restrictive qualifying conditions.

Economic standard of living in New Zealand

The following information on the economic standard of living in New Zealand is taken from *The Social Report* (Ministry of Social Policy, 2001), which is online at www.msp.govt.nz.

Key points of The Social Report 2001 *concerning standard of living*

- **Market income per person** grew slowly from 1986 to 1989, then declined until 1992 before rising again.
- **Income inequality** has increased over the past decade, mainly due to a larger overall rise in the incomes of high-income earners.
- Data on **low incomes** shows an increase in the proportion of the population experiencing low incomes between 1988 and 1994.
  - Between 1994 and 1998 (the most recently available data), the proportion of the population with low incomes has decreased, but remains well above 1988 levels.
  - The incidence of low incomes is particularly high for sole parent families, those reliant on benefit incomes, households composed of young couples with children, those living in rented accommodation and for Pacific peoples, Maori and the 'Other' ethnic groups.
- One quarter of households pay **housing costs** greater than 30% of their income, a proportion that rose over the decade from 1988 to 1998.
- **Household crowding** affects 3.4% of the population, including 5.3% of all children. Maori and Pacific people have a much higher probability of living in a crowded household than other ethnic groups.
- Self-reported **food insecurity** affected 13% of New Zealand households in 1997, particularly among Maori and Pacific peoples.
- 8.1% of the population regarded their household's standard of living as 'low' or 'fairly low'. This was especially true of sole parent households.

Summary of findings to 1998

New Zealand's overall income has increased since 1988. However, this increase has not been reflected in the economic standard of living of all New Zealanders. Income inequality increased over the decade from 1988 to 1998. Working age families rather than the retired population seem to have the most difficulty.

Measures of economic standards of living

New Zealand has no official poverty measure. However, a number of different unofficial measures of poverty or economic hardship can provide insights into different aspects of economic standard of living.

One such measure is the Real Gross National Disposable Income (RGNDI). This is a measure of the total volume of goods and services available to New Zealanders for consumption. Because it is a measure of volume it is not affected by inflation.

- In 1986, RGNDI per person was $20,097 (1991/92 dollars). In 2000, RGNDI per person was $23,086 (1991/2 dollars). This represents an average growth rate over the period of just under 1% per year.
- RGNDI grew slowly between 1986 and 1989, before falling to below its 1986 level by 1992.
- Since 1992, there has been steady growth, except for 1998–99.

International comparisons

Comparisons with 26 other OECD countries are available for the slightly different measure, real gross domestic product (GDP) per person.

Between 1986 and 1999, real GDP per person grew by 9.5% compared with an OECD average growth of 29%.

New Zealand's OECD ranking for GDP

1970	9th
1986	18th
1999	20th

Social Welfare expenditure

Social welfare spending (Vote Social Development) by the government has been budgeted for $13,904.887 million in the 2002/03 financial year, or 36% of total government expenditure.

Benefits costs as share of total government expenditure

New Zealand Super	14%
Unemployment	3%
Domestic purposes	4%
Other benefits	15%

Of this total, $11,898.840 million (85.57% of the Vote) is for benefits and other unrequited expenses, including:

- New Zealand Superannuation ($5645.200 million) to approximately 454,000 New Zealanders.
- Unemployment Benefit ($1364.409 million) to approximately 134,000 New Zealanders.
- Domestic Purposes Benefit ($1521.094 million) to approximately 110,000 New Zealanders.
- Student Allowance ($440.982 million) to approximately 60,000 students.
- Other social security benefits ($2927.155 million).

In addition, $1152.098 million (8.29% of the Vote) is for capital contributions including:

- Student Loans ($1052.049 million) to approximately 159,000 students.

- Recoverable Assistance to low-income households ($99.569 million).

During the 2000/2001 financial year, total benefit and pension expenditure (including New Zealand Superannuation and War Pensions) was $11,910 million. Of this expenditure, New Zealand Superannuation accounted for $5390 million and War Pensions $103 million.

Strategies for children and youth

The Ministry of Social Development has developed an Agenda for Children to raise children's status in society and promote a 'whole child' approach to developing government policy and services affecting children. Its vision statement is 'New Zealand/Aotearoa is a great place for children: we look after one another'.

The Ministry is also the lead agency in the collaborative 'Strengthening Families' strategy that includes the Ministries of Health and Education and other government and community agencies.

The Ministry of Youth Affairs concentrates its activities on improving the lives of young people in five key areas: learning; working and earning; well-being; families and youth at risk; and citizenship.

The Ministry of Youth Affairs released its *Youth Development Strategy Aotearoa* in February 2002, which is available on its website www.youthaffairs.govt.nz.

The youth development approach is similar and complementary to the whole child approach of the Agenda for Children, but is for the older age group (from 12 to 24 years inclusive).

Health

Summary and OECD comparisons of health data

- Life expectancy at birth:
  - 75.7 years for males and 80.8 years for females (1998–2000).
  - Lower for Maori and Pacific peoples. Variation between regions.
  - Steadily improving.
  - Average compared with OECD.
- Dependent disability:
  - 11% of the population have a disability requiring assistance (1996–97).
  - Higher rates among people aged 65 years and above and Maori.
- Life expectancy:
  - 64.6 years for males and 67.9 years for females (1996).
  - Lower for males and Maori.
- Infant mortality:
  - The infant mortality rate in New Zealand has generally declined since the 1930s.
  - Recent improvements are thought to be due to the decline in sudden infant death syndrome (SIDS), from changes in the way babies are put to sleep.
  - In 1998 the Maori and Pacific infant mortality rates were almost twice as high as for European/Other.
  - New Zealand ranking for infant mortality rates was 19 of 27 OECD countries for which 1999 data was available.
- Youth suicide:
  - 26.1 suicides per 100,000 young people aged 15–24 (1998).
  - Much higher rates for young men and for Maori but more attempted suicides by young women.

  - Worsening to 1996 then stable.
  - Very poor compared with OECD.
- Births to young adolescents:
  - 8.8 births per 1000 young women aged 13–17 (2000).
  - Rates higher for Maori but declining faster. Variation between regions.
  - Improving since mid-1990s.
  - Poor compared with OECD.
- Prevalence of cigarette smoking:
  - 25% of population aged 15 and over smoke cigarettes (2000).
  - Higher rates among young people, Maori, Pacific peoples and those living in deprived areas.
  - Improving to 1991, steady since.
  - Good for males, average for females compared with OECD.

Health system structure

The New Zealand health system is made up of public, private and voluntary sectors, which interact to provide and fund health care. Over 75% of health care is publicly funded. For more details see *An Overview of the Health and Disability Sector in New Zealand* (Ministry of Health, November 2001) on www.moh.govt.nz.

For general information on the health system in New Zealand and how to use it, see www.everybody.co.nz.

Ministry of Health

The Ministry of Health advises the government on health and disability support services, and carries out the government's policies in these areas. This involves a range of activities such as funding, planning, and monitoring health services either directly or through the district health boards (DHBs).

District health boards

On 1 January 2001, the government created 21 district health boards. These are responsible for planning, funding and providing government-funded health care services for their local populations, within capped budgets.

Auckland	www.adhb.govt.nz
Bay of Plenty	www.bopdhb.govt.nz
Canterbury	www.cdhb.govt.nz
Capital & Coast	www.ccdhb.org.nz
Counties-Manukau	www.cmdhb.org.nz
Hawke's Bay	www.hawkesbaydhb.govt.nz
Hutt Valley	www.huttvalleydhb.org.nz
Lakes	www.lhl.co.nz
MidCentral	www.midcentral.co.nz
Nelson-Marlborough	www.nmdhb.govt.nz
Northland	www.nhl.co.nz
Otago	www.otagodhb.govt.nz
South Canterbury	www.scdhb.co.nz
Southland	www.southlandhealth.co.nz
Taranaki	www.tdhb.org.nz
Waikato	www.waikatodhb.govt.nz
Wairarapa	wairarapa.dhb.org.nz
Waitemata	www.whl.co.nz
West Coast	www.westcoastdhb.org.nz
Whanganui	www.wdhb.org.nz

In the 2002/03 budget $36 million was dedicated to funding a vaccine programme for meningoccocal meningitis.

Expenditure on health

Health spending trends to 1999

- From 1991/92 to 1998/99 real per capita public expenditure steadily rose by an average $35 a year, from $1290 to $1530 (19th in the OECD).
- Vote Health remained steady during the early to mid 1990s at about 5.5% of the Gross Domestic Product (GDP). It jumped to 5.8% in 1997/98 and 6.3% in 1998/99.

Budgeted government health spending (Vote Health) for 2002/03

Health care and disability spending by the government (Vote Health) has been budged for $8,645.493 million, or 20% of total government spending in the 2002/03 budget. This total is an increase of $940.846 million or 12.2% from 2001/02. The main areas of spending within this amount are:

- $5,411.379 million (63% of Vote Health) to purchase health services from DHBs.
- $1,421.738 million (16.5% of Vote Health) to purchase national disability support services.
- $715.066 million (8% of Vote Health) to provide capital funding and loan facilities for DHBs.
- $518.914 million (6% of Vote Health) to purchase national health services.
- $221.682 million (2.6% of Vote Health) to purchase public health services.
- $166.917 million (2% of Vote Health) to the Ministry of Health Income for 2002/03 budget.
- The Ministry expects to collect $292.005 million of Crown revenue in 2002/03, most of which is the reimbursement of accident-related acute public hospital costs from the Accident Rehabilitation and Compensation Insurance Corporation and insurers.

Major health issues

Causes of illness and health

Health is affected by a number of different factors. Some examples of particular importance in New Zealand are:

- Socioeconomic factors such as unemployment. The unemployment rate has dropped from 10% in 1991 to 5.2% in 2001. However, unemployment is higher among Maori (12.3%) and Pacific people (10%) than Europeans (4%).
- Environmental factors. Nearly all New Zealanders have drinking water that has been tested for safety, and 62% receive fluoridated water to prevent tooth decay.
- 'Biological risk factors' such as obesity. There has been a 50% increase in adult obesity in the last decade. In 1997 over half of all adults were overweight or obese.
- Behaviour.
  - Smoking is still by far the main cause of preventable deaths.
  - Participation in physical activities. Some 61–67% of adults are physically active.
  - Diet: in 1997 less than half of all adults ate enough vegetables and fruit, and an average 15% of energy in their diets was from saturated fats.
  - Alcohol: New Zealand has a moderate to low alcohol consumption compared to other OECD countries, but from 1995 to 2000 much more alcohol was drunk by young people.

Health issues by age

Each age group has a different set of health problems. Some of the major challenges at each age are:

Children (under 15 years old)

- Injuries
- Mental health
- Respiratory illnesses

Young People

- Injuries
- Mental health

Adults

- Cardiovascular disease
- Cancers

Currently over 110,000 people in New Zealand are diagnosed with diabetes and it is estimated that the same number of people might be affected but are undiagnosed. The disease causes more than 1500 deaths each year; with complications including heart disease, blindness, kidney failure and lower limb amputations. The disease is three times more common in Maori and Pacific people and by 2011 the number of Maori people with diabetes is expected to have nearly doubled.

Hospitalisation

From 1988 to 1997 rates of admission to hospitals increased by about 24% for males and 30% for females. This could be due to people surviving more life-threatening conditions for longer, greater availability of hospital care, and changing patterns in referrals from GPs.

The threat of widespread bubonic plague led to the establishment of a Department of Public Health in 1901. In fact the worst plague in New Zealand history was the 1918 influenza epidemic which killed 8500 people.

Accidents

ACC

The Accident Compensation Corporation (ACC) administers New Zealand's accident compensation scheme, which provides accident insurance for all New Zealand citizens, residents and temporary visitors to New Zealand. In return people do not have the right to sue for personal injury, other than for exemplary damages.

- ACC manages about 1.4 million injury claims every year.
- ACC paid nearly $1.3 billion in expenditure for compensation, rehabilitation, and medical treatment in the year ending 30 June 2001.
- 15 to 19-year-old males had the highest number of new claims; 35 to 39-year-old males were the most costly.
- 4% of new entitlement claims covered by ACC were the result of a motor vehicle accident.
- 28% of new claims covered by ACC in the year to 30 June 2001 were the result of injuries occurring in the home.
- Weekly compensation for time off work was the largest expenditure category in the year ending 30 June 2001, making up 47% of all expenditure.

Traffic accidents (year to June)

	1998	2000
Road deaths	501	462
Deaths/10,000 vehicles	2.2	1.8
Deaths/100,000 people	13.2	12.1
Reported injuries	12 412	10 962
Reported injuries/10,000 vehicles	54	42
Reported injuries/100,000 people	327	286
Number hospitalised (discharges)	6 260	5 960
Cyclists killed	16	19
Pedestrians killed	71	35

There has been a big improvement in drink-driving crash rates over the last 15 years. In the late 1980s about 40% (over 150 drivers a year) of all the drivers killed had a blood alcohol level above the legal limit. In 2001 just over 20%, (or 55 drivers) were killed while drink-driving.

Road toll data

The year 2001 saw the lowest annual road toll in 37 years:

- The provisional road toll for 2001 was at 455, a drop of seven on 2000 and the lowest annual toll since 1964, when 428 were killed.
- The last time a road toll lower than 455 was recorded was 1964, when New Zealand's population was 2.6 million and 964,000 vehicles were on the roads. (With a road toll of 428 in 1964, there were 4.4 deaths for every 10,000 vehicles.)
- In 2001, the population had grown to 3.8 million and the number of vehicles to a record 2.6 million.
- With the provisional toll of 455 in 2001, the death rate has shrunk to 1.7 deaths per 10,000 vehicles.
- Had the 2001 fatality rate last year been the same as in 1964, the road toll would have been 1159.
- Had the fatality rates of 1973 continued (5.9 deaths per 10,000 vehicles), a staggering 1553 people would have died on the roads last year.

Ten most common crash factors

1. Too fast for conditions
2. Alcohol
3. Failed to give way
4. Road factors
5. Did not see other party
6. Inattention or attention diverted
7. Driver tired or fell asleep
8. Pedestrian factors
9. Inexperienced
10. Vehicle factors

Note: Factors are measured by social cost. Calculations include loss of life or life quality, loss of output due to injuries, medical and rehabilitation costs, legal and court costs and property damage.

International comparisons: motor accident death rates (1999)

	Killed	Per 100,000 pop.	Per 10,000 vehicles
Australia	1 759	9.3	1.4
Canada	2 972	9.7	1.7
France	8 487	14.4	2.5
Germany	7 772	9.5	1.5
Japan	10 372	8.2	1.3
NZ	509	13.3	2.0
Spain	5 738	14.6	2.6
Sweden	580	6.6	1.3
UK	3 564	6.0	1.3
USA	41 611	15.3	2.0

The 2002 national survey of front seatbelt use by adults found that men are twice as likely to neglect to buckle up as women. Some 10% of male drivers and 12% of male passengers observed in the survey were unrestrained, compared to just 5% of female drivers and passengers. Police attending crashes in 2001 estimated that at least 29 of the 86 unrestrained vehicle occupants killed could have survived had they been buckled up.

Water accidents

Water Safety New Zealand (www.watersafety.org.nz) is the national organisation responsible for ensuring that all New Zealanders are safe in and around water at home, in public pools, at the beach, in lakes, in rivers or out at sea.

An extensive coastline and numerous waterways make water sports and recreation among the most popular activities. However, per capita accidental deaths by drowning are high.

Numbers drowned

1991	147
1995	154
2001	115

International comparison: drownings (rates per 100,000 person years, 1998)

Norway	4.7	Australia	2.2
France	4.2	US	1.9
New Zealand	3.7	Israel	1.2

General accident statistics

In 1995, 1996 and 1997, accidents, poisonings and violence accounted for 6% of deaths from all causes. The most common single external cause of death in 1997 was suicide and self-inflicted injury (561 deaths), followed by motor vehicle crashes (550 deaths) and accidental falls (242 deaths).

Fatal accidents investigated by Occupational Health & Safety (1 July 2001 to 30 June 2002)

Industrial/Commercial	29	(6 homicides)
Construction	12	(6 from a fall)
Forestry	2	(1 from felling)
Agriculture	25	(7 ATV)
Mines and Quarries	5	
Total	**73**	

The New Zealand Fire Service

The New Zealand Fire Service is involved both in fighting fires and preventing them. It comprises approximately:

- 1690 career fire fighters (20 females).

- 8000 urban volunteer fire fighters (440 females).
- 3000 rural volunteer and part-time fire fighters.
- eight fire regions comprising: 348 fire districts (urban); 435 fire stations.
- 800 fire appliances (approx.).

Fire statistics

	Fires	Total calls	Fatalities
1999–00	19 922	59 238	32
1998–99	21 475	64 057	42
1997–98	24 291	61 730	47
1996–97	20 553	54 307	52
1995–96	17 884	46 553	32

Youth suicide

Suicide is the second leading cause of death among 15 to 24 year olds in New Zealand (after motor vehicle accidents). Almost one in four people who died by suicide in 1998 were aged between 15 and 24 years old. Males and Maori are disproportionately represented in the statistics.

New Zealand has a high rate of youth suicide compared to the rates of other countries. However, this information has to be interpreted with caution, as different countries classify suicide under different health code headings.

Youth suicide deaths, by sex and ethnicity, 1999 (provisional)

	Total	Maori	Non-Maori
Both sexes	119	33	86
Males	82	23	59
Females	37	10	27

Number of youth suicide deaths (1980–99)

	Total	Males	Females
1980	81	58	23
1982	63	52	11
1984	72	57	15
1986	91	68	23
1988	131	106	25
1990	130	111	19
1992	129	112	17
1994	137	111	26
1996	143	105	38
1998	140	105	35
1999*	119	82	37

* Provisional.

Drug abuse

Alcohol

- The 1995 National Alcohol Survey showed 87% of 14 to 65 year olds consumed alcohol in the previous 12 months.
- In 1998 there were 26,512 prosecutions for traffic offences involving alcohol. Approximately 91% (24,059) of these prosecutions resulted in a conviction.
- There were 142 deaths in 1997 where the underlying cause was an alcohol-related condition, including heart and liver damage, high blood pressure, some types of cancer and digestive disorders. Alcohol-related conditions account for 3.1% of all male deaths and 1.41% of female.
- 10% of deaths due to external causes (e.g. falls, motor vehicle accidents, suicide) involved a positive blood alcohol concentration in the deceased.

- 11% of female drivers and 21% of males involved in fatal car crashes in 1996–98 period had alcohol involvement.
- Overall, drinking drivers contributed to 23% of all fatal motor vehicle accidents and 14% of all injury motor vehicle accidents in the year ended December 1999.
- Alcohol was involved in 19% of all drownings over the period 1980–99.
- There were 8551 publicly funded hospitalisations in 1998 where a diagnosis of an alcohol-related condition or alcohol involvement was made.
- Alcohol-related hospitalisations are estimated to cost New Zealand more than $74 million each year.
- At some time in their life, nearly one in five New Zealanders will suffer an alcohol use disorder.

Drink driving is responsible for almost one in three deaths of rural people in road crashes.

Smoking

General trends and facts

- Smoking decreased by about 2% from the early 1990s to 2000. This represents about 55,000 fewer smokers.
- This decrease, however, is not true for those aged 15 to 24.
- This decrease is also not true for Maori and Pacific peoples.
- From 1997 to 2000, the number of cigarettes smoked per smoker per day decreased from 13 to 12.
- In 2000, about one quarter of 15 to 19 year olds and about a third of those aged 20 to 24 claimed to be smokers.
- Those on low incomes were most likely to smoke.

Ethnicity rates of smoking in 2000

- Europeans/others: just over one in five (21.9%).
- Pacific peoples: around one in three (33.9%).
- Maori: one in two (49.3%).

In recent years there have been a number of tobacco control initiatives including a multi-media campaign. The national freephone Quitline (0800 778 778) has operated since mid-1998. Callers can request a pack of quit smoking materials, and talk to a Quit Advisor for support and advice.

Preventable future deaths

- Using different methods, the number of total deaths due to smoking is estimated as between approximately 4300 and 4700 annually.
- It is estimated that in New Zealand many deaths due to various diseases could be prevented if smoking was eliminated, including:
  - 68% of female deaths and 82% of male deaths due to lung cancer.
  - 65% of female deaths and 79% of male deaths due to chronic obstructive respiratory disease.
  - 11% of female deaths and 18% of male deaths due to heart disease.
  - 8% of female deaths and 15% of male deaths due to strokes.
- Each year, 21% of deaths in female Maori are attributable to smoking and 22% of male Maori deaths.

According to some research, there are about 388 deaths caused by second-hand cigarette smoke in New Zealand each year, the equivalent of an extra 8% over and above deaths due to direct smoking.

Cannabis

- Marijuana or cannabis, although illegal, is the third most popular recreational drug in New Zealand after alcohol and tobacco (excluding caffeine).

- In the 1998 National Drugs Survey, 43% of males and 27% of females aged 18 to 24 years had used marijuana in the preceding 12 months. Most of those who stated that they had tried marijuana had been introduced to the drug at between 14 and 18 years of age.
- There were seven deaths over the period 1990–96 where a cannabis-related condition such as drug abuse or dependence was the underlying cause of death.
- There were 2722 cannabis-related hospitalisations over the period 1996–98.

Other illicit drugs

- Opium and its derivatives had been tried by 4% of surveyed respondents in the 1998 National Drug Survey.
- 13% of National Drug Survey respondents in 1998 stated that they had tried hallucinogens at some time. In the Regional Drugs Surveys, the percentage of 18 to 24 year olds that had used LSD in the previous year grew from 5% in 1990 to 11% in 1998.
- There were 156 deaths in the period 1990–96 where opiate-related conditions or poisonings were the underlying cause of death.
- Over the three-year period 1996–98 there were 3955 opiate-related publicly funded hospitalisations.

Other drugs

- In the 1998 National Drug Survey, approximately 2% of those surveyed stated that they had tried tranquillisers for recreational purposes, with a similar proportion having ever tried solvents.
- There were 148 deaths in the period 1990–96 where depressant-related conditions were the underlying cause of death. Thirty-five of these deaths were specifically due to solvents.

- Over the three-year period 1996–98 there were 9271 publicly funded hospitalisations that involved depressant-related conditions and/or poisoning by a depressant as the reason for admission or as a secondary diagnosis. Of these hospitalisations, 531 involved a solvent-related condition and/or poisoning.

The National Poison Centre in Dunedin fields about 20,000 phone calls per year.

Dental health

New Zealand's dental health service comprises:

- Free school dental care for children.
- Dental benefits for adolescents (up to 16 for all, up to 18 for those in study).
- Private practice for adults.
- Hospital services for inpatients and other special groups.

For children leaving primary school the average number of filled teeth was 1.6 per child, and 44% had no fillings in their permanent teeth.

Sexual health

- A Dunedin study estimated that the median age for first sexual intercourse was 17 for males and 16 for females. No information is available for young gay males or females.
- New Zealand has a higher total fertility rate than other OECD countries.
- Rates of birth to teenage mothers (15–19 years) are higher than most other OECD countries (the notable exception being the US).
- Sexually transmitted infections (STI) rates are increasing, particularly among those under 24.
- Chlamydia is the most common STI.

- AIDS (acquired immune deficiency syndrome) cases have decreased since peaking over 1989–96, due to advances in HIV (human immunodeficiency virus) medications.

Abortions

Abortion is legal in certain circumstances under the Contraception, Sterilisation and Abortion Act 1977. The main conditions are that continuing the pregnancy would result in serious danger to the physical or mental health of the woman, or that there is a strong likelihood that the child would be seriously mentally or physically handicapped.

- Increasing numbers of abortions are being performed. Just over one in five known pregnancies were terminated by induced abortion in the year ending December 2000.
- There are now more repeat abortions.
- A growing proportion of women having abortions have already had one or more live births. Pregnancies are being terminated earlier, most commonly at 10 weeks.

New Zealand abortion rates compared

International comparisons are affected by both how each country measures its rates, and the differences in their laws. The following must be interpreted with care. (Rate is per 1000 estimated mean number of women 15–44 years.)

United States	22.9
Australia	22.2
New Zealand	19.0
Sweden	18.1
Canada, England, Wales	16.1
Finland	10.5
Germany	8.0
The Netherlands	7.4

Mortality

Major causes of death

Malignant neoplasms (cancer), ischaemic heart disease and cerebrovascular disease were the leading causes of death in New Zealand from 1997 to 1999. In 1999 they collectively accounted for almost 60% of deaths:

- cancer 27%
- ischaemic heart disease 23%
- cerebrovascular disease 10%.

Deathly disasters in New Zealand history

1863	HMS *Orpheus* shipwrecked; 189 died.
1863	Fierce winter conditions killed over 100 goldminers in Central Otago.
1865	The *Fiery Star* caught fire; 78 lost at sea.
1866	The *General Grant*, carrying gold bullion, was wrecked on the Auckland Islands; 15 survived the wreck; 10 survived 18 months until rescued.
1879	Coal mine explosion in Kaitangata, Otago; 35 killed.
1881	The *Tararua* wrecked near Slope Point, Southland; 131 of 151 died.
1886	Mt Tarawera erupted; at least 106 killed, some estimates up to 153. Destruction of the famous pink and white terraces.
1894	The *Wairarapa* rammed full steam into Great Barrier Island; 135 of 230 onboard died.
1896	Fire in the Brunner mine on the West Coast killed 67 men.
1902	The *Elingamite* hit rocks off the Three Kings Island; 45 of 195 onboard died.
1909	The *Penguin* was guided into Cook Strait by the famous dolphin Pelorus Jack, but struck rocks off Cape Terawhiti; 75 of 105 onboard died.
1914	Explosion in Ralph's mine at Huntly; 43 killed.

1917	Battle of Passchendaele; 640 killed, 2100 wounded in one day.
1918	Influenza epidemic; estimated 8500 died.
1918	The *Wimmera* hit a German mine; 27 drowned.
1923	Train crashed into a landslide 32 km north of Taumarunui; 17 killed.
1929	Murchison earthquake; 17 killed.
1931	Napier/Hawke's Bay earthquake; 256 killed.
1938	Flash flood drowned 21 in a railway construction camp at Kopuawhara, near the isthmus of Mahia Peninsula. Thousands of sheep and cattle also drowned.
1939	Fire at the Glen Afton mine, Huntly; 11 died.
1942	Fire at Seacliff Mental Hospital, 36 km north of Dunedin; 37 of 39 trapped women died.
1943	Train jumped the track 5 km past Hyde in Otago; 21 passengers killed.
1947	Fire at Ballantyne's Store in Christchurch; 41 staff died.
1948	Aeroplane crashed into Mt Ruapehu; 13 killed.
1949	Aeroplane crashed into Tararua foothills; 15 killed.
1953	Wellington to Auckland express train plunged into the Whangaehu River at Tangiwai when the bridge was swept away by a flood of silt and water from the crater lake on Mt Ruapehu. 151 were killed, on Christmas Eve.
1963	Bus crash killed 15, injured 21, returning from Waitangi celebrations.
1967	Explosion at the Strongman mine near Greymouth; 19 killed.
1968	The ferry *Wahine* sank off Wellington, 51 drowned.
1979	Air New Zealand DC 10 crashed into Mt Erebus, in the Antarctic; 257 killed.
1990	David Gray shot and killed 13 in Aramoana, near Dunedin.
1995	Viewing platform at Cave Creek on the West Coast collapsed; 14 young people killed.

Education

(All information below comes from the Ministry of Education and the Ministry for Social Development unless otherwise indicated. See www.minedu.govt.nz and 'The Social Report 2001' on www.msd.govt.nz.)

Summary and OECD comparisons

(A summary and comparisons of knowledge and skills indicators.)

- Participation in early childhood education:
  - 'Apparent' participation rate of 92% for three year olds and 100% for four year olds (2000). Maori rates lower than non-Maori.
  - Trend improving.
  - Good compared with OECD.
- School leavers with higher school qualifications:
  - 66% of school leavers with at least Sixth Form Certificate (1999). Proportions lower for males, Maori and Pacific young people.
  - Improving to 1991, steady since.
- Educational attainment of the adult population:
  - 71.1% of the population aged 25–64 years with at least an upper secondary qualification (2000). Proportions lower for older people, women as well as Maori and Pacific peoples.
  - Trend improving.
  - Average compared with OECD.
- Adult literacy skills in English:
  - Various international agencies state that 99% of the population aged 15 and over can read and write sufficiently to meet the complex demands of everyday life and work.
  - Literacy levels lower among older people, Maori and Pacific peoples and other ethnic groups.

- Compared with OECD: average on document literacy and quantitative; good on prose.

- Participation in tertiary education:
  - 9% of population aged 16 and over enrolled in tertiary education institutions (2000). Lower rates for males, students from poorer socio-economic communities, and those aged above 25.
  - Trend improving slowly.
  - Good compared with OECD.

Additional notes:

- Participation rates in early childhood education have been steadily improving, especially for Maori and Pacific children.
- The proportion of school leavers with higher school qualifications improved in the late 1980s, but has since been stable.
- The level of educational attainment of adults in the population improved throughout the 1990s.
- New Zealand has internationally high rates of participation in tertiary education with nearly a quarter of 16 to 24 year olds enrolled in a tertiary institution.

Some important dates in education

1847	Ordinance setting aside 5% of colony's revenue for education.
1852	Provincial councils funding schools.
1867	Native Schools Act – village schools for Maori.
1869	University of New Zealand (Otago) founded.
1877	Education Act: free compulsory schooling for all European 7 to 13 year olds.
1903	Free compulsory education extended to all Maori children.
	High schools to provide 20% of their places for free.
1914	Free high schooling to all children passing proficiency exam.

1936	Access to high school automatic and free up to 19.
1940s	Kindergarten movement supported by government training. Playcentre movement begins.
1944	Leaving age raised to 15.
1975	Private Schools Conditional Integration Act.
1982	First Kohanga Reo centre opened.
1989	'Tomorrow's Schools' reorganisation of sector begins.
1992	Student loan scheme for tertiary students established.
1993	School leaving age raised to 16. Wananga recognised as state Maori tertiary institutions.
1999	Students enrolled at approved private tertiary education providers granted state funding.
2000	Changes to the composition of the polytechnic and university sectors.
2002	Introduction of the controversial National Certificate of Educational Achievement to replace School Certificate.

Education agencies

The Ministry of Education has many roles: policy advice and implementation, providing funding, monitoring and managing education resources, administering legislation, carrying out research and developing national guidelines.

Other agencies are:

- Early Childhood Development www.ecd.govt.nz
- Specialist Education Services www.ses.org.nz
- Career Services www.careers.govt.nz
- Educ. & Training Support Agency www.skillnz.govt.nz
- NZ Qualifications Authority www.nzqa.govt.nz
- Education Review Office www.ero.govt.nz
- Learning Media Ltd www.learningmedia.co.nz
- Teacher Registration Board www.trb.govt.nz

School management

Boards of trustees govern all state and integrated schools in New Zealand. The boards are made up of elected parent and community volunteers, the school principal and a staff representative. Secondary school boards must also have a student representative.

Committees, trustee boards and management boards acting on behalf of the owners govern independent schools.

All schools are required to ensure they provide equal educational opportunity for their students and respect for the diverse ethnic and cultural heritage of New Zealand people.

Student rolls snapshot

	1999	2000	2001
Primary	481 183	484 161	484 058
Secondary	246 213	245 528	249 866
Polytechnic	98 451	100 037	87 855
University	105 996	122 727	125 547
College of Education	12 793	12 045	10 894
Wananga (Maori tertiary institutions)	1 883	2 972	11 281

Government expenditure on education

Education spending by the government (Vote Education) was budgeted for $7,513.692 million or 18% of total government expenditure in the 2002/03 financial year.

- Want to know more about teaching in New Zealand? See www.TeachNZ.govt.nz.
- Want to know about studying in New Zealand? See www.educationnz.org.nz.

Vote Education spending 2001–02 ($ billion)

Compulsory education	3.73
Post compulsory education	1.70
School property	1.02
Early childhood	0.39
Other outputs	0.17
Total spending	**7.01**

Compulsory education spending 2001–02 ($ billion)

Primary education	1.83
Secondary education	1.27
Special education	0.35
Professional and curriculum support	0.12
School transport	0.11
Other	0.05
Total spending	**3.73**

School terms

- Primary schools must be open for at least 394 half days each year.
- Secondary schools must be open for at least 380 half days each year.
- In 1996, schools moved from three terms to four terms per year (four holiday breaks).
- Summer holidays are six weeks; the others are two weeks.

Studies showed that students became less tired and were able to concentrate and work better when terms were shorter and holiday breaks more frequent.

Early childhood education

There are many different early childhood services. The main ones are:

- Kindergartens
- Playcentres
- Kohanga Reo (Maori language nests)
- Pacific Islands language groups
- Anau Ako Pasifika (development project)
- Education and care centres
- Home-based services (family daycare)
- Playgroups
- Parents as First Teachers (PAFT)

Attendance for early childhood education:

- From July 1990 to July 2001 the overall number of institutions has grown by 46% and the overall number of enrolments has increased by almost 45%.
- Apparent participation of 0 to 4 year olds has increased from 42% in 1990 to 60% in 2001.
- Results from the schools July 2001 collection indicate that around 91% of new entrants had attended Early Childhood Education as 4 year olds.

Levels of schooling

Compulsory education in New Zealand is divided into primary, intermediate and secondary schooling:

- Primary schools cater for children from the age of five years (Year 0) to the end of Year 6.
- Children in Years 7 and 8 may either be in a separate intermediate school or part of a primary, secondary or composite/area school.
- Secondary schools usually provide for students from Year 9 until the end of Year 13.

Area/composite schools are usually in rural areas, and combine primary, intermediate and secondary schooling in one location.

Types of schools

- State schools are attended by most children. These are coeducational at primary and intermediate levels, but may be single sex at secondary level. Some offer adult education.
- Integrated schools follow the state curriculum requirements but incorporate their own special character into the school programme (usually religious). State funding is received for pupils but schools meet their own building and land costs.
- Kura Kaupapa Maori (Maori medium schools) are state schools where teaching is in Maori language, and based on Maori culture. The curriculum is the same as other state schools.
- Independent (private) schools charge fees but also receive some state funding. They must meet certain state standards to be registered.
- Boarding schools may be independent or state-funded, but both charge boarding fees.
- The Correspondence School is a national school providing distance courses for early childhood, primary, secondary and adult students. (See www.correspondence.school.nz)
- Home-based schooling is allowed, provided parents maintain a standard equal to that of a registered school. Parents receive a grant to help with schooling costs.

The number of homeschooled children increased substantially from 1993 to 2001, from 2738 to 5976. From 2000 to 2001 this growth slowed with only 99 new homeschoolers.

The curriculum

The New Zealand Curriculum Framework specifies seven essential learning areas:

- Language and languages
- Mathematics
- Science
- Technology
- Social sciences
- The arts
- Health and physical well-being

Essential skills to be developed in the context of these areas are:

- Communication
- Numeracy
- Information
- Problem-solving
- Self-management and competitive
- Social and cooperative
- Physical
- Work and study

Literacy and numeracy are key goals.

Every school day around 100,000 children go to school on approximately 2300 school bus services. About another 10,000 students receive transport allowances.

National qualifications

From 2002, a new set of national qualifications, The National Certificate of Educational Achievement (NCEA), replaced the previous certificates.

Students are able to achieve the NCEA via a wide range of courses and subjects, within and beyond the school curriculum. The qualification looks to remove the old distinctions between academic and vocational training. For example, in the subject of science, research skills are recognised along with the more academic learning.

In each school curriculum subject there is both external assessment (including examinations) and internal assessment (where the school awards grades).

NCEA timetable

2002	NCEA Level 1 replaces School Certificate
2003	NCEA Level 2 replaces Sixth Form Certificate
2004	NCEA Levels 3 and 4 replace University Bursaries

There will also be a scholarship award for high achieving school leavers.

The National Qualifications Framework

The Qualifications Framework covers industry and education qualifications from Year 11 (formerly Form 5) of secondary schooling and entry level to vocations, through to post-graduate level. This means students can start on Framework qualifications at school and carry on in the workplace or tertiary studies. They can work on specific National Certificates and Diplomas as well as the general NCEA.

International students

- There were 11,332 international students attending schools at 1 July 2001.
- The number of foreign fee-paying (FFP) students has continued to increase markedly from 7191 in July 2000 to 10,555 in July 2001, an increase of 46.8% (3364 students).
- This group accounts for 1.4% of the school population.
- Over 95% of this increase came from the Asian region.
- Increasing numbers of primary aged FFP students are attending schools. In 2001 there were 1823 FFP students in Years 1 to 8, compared with 507 in 1999.

Revenue generated by foreign students exceeded $1 billion in the year ending June 2001, up from $540 million in 1999. The economic benefit generated by overseas students includes fees, accommodation, living costs and spending on tourism.

Tertiary education

Formal tertiary education is study undertaken at a public or private tertiary education provider that leads to a recognised New Zealand qualification. Public tertiary education institutions include universities, polytechnics, colleges of education and wananga.

In 2000 there were 38 public tertiary institutions from which 60,645 students graduated with a total of 63,487 awards. There are also 215 private tertiary education providers which receive Ministry funding or are eligible for loans and allowances.

In 2000 there were 13,947 students who graduated with a total of 14,260 awards.

Public providers (2002)

Polytechnics

Aoraki Polytechnic
Bay of Plenty Polytechnic
Christchurch Polytechnic Institute of Technology
Eastern Institute of Technology
Manukau Institute of Technology
Nelson Marlborough Institute of Technology
Northland Polytechnic
Open Polytechnic of New Zealand
Otago Polytechnic
Southern Institute of Technology
Tai Poutini Polytechnic
Tairawhiti Polytechnic

Taranaki Polytechnic
Telford Rural Polytechnic
Unitec Institute of Technology
Universal College of Learning
Waiariki Institute of Technology
Waikato Institute of Technology
Wanganui Regional Community Polytechnic
Wellington Institute of Technology
Whitireia Community Polytechnic

Colleges of Education
Auckland College Of Education
Christchurch College of Education
Dunedin College of Education
Wellington College of Education

Universities
Auckland University of Technology
Lincoln University
Massey University
University of Auckland
University of Canterbury
University of Otago
University of Waikato
Victoria University of Wellington

Wananga
Te Wananga O Aotearoa
Te Wananga O Raukawa
Te Whare Wananga O Awanuiarangi

Wananga provide tertiary education and training, while assisting the application of knowledge regarding Maori tradition in accordance with Maori custom.

Tertiary qualifications

Tertiary students and awards (1996–2000)

	Students	% growth	Awards	% growth
1996	47 623	–	49 589	–
1997	54 325	14.1%	56 000	12.9%
1998	57 594	6.0%	59 465	6.2%
1999	60 098	4.3%	62 711	5.5%
2000	60 645	0.9%	63 487	1.2%

Thirty-six percent of the completed qualifications were awarded at the certificate level, 11% at the diploma level, 38% at the degree level, and 15% at the post-graduate level.

Completed tertiary qualifications (1998–2000)

Award Group	1998	1999	2000
Doctorate	407	476	464
Masters/Honours	4 720	5 304	5 093
Post-Grad. Dip./Cert.	3 388	3 491	3 814
Bachelors/Advanced Dip.	21 514	23 677	24 117
Diploma	7 866	7 019	7 169
Certificate	21 570	22 744	22 830
Total	**59 465**	**62 711**	**63 487**

- Maori participation in tertiary education has increased rapidly, more than doubling between 1991 and 1997.
- The number of Maori graduates (7859) has increased by 26% from 1997 to 2000, although there was a slight decrease from 1999 to 2000.
- This pattern matches the overall trend in the numbers of students completing qualifications over the last four years.
- Maori graduates now make up 12% of all graduates.

Field of study

The largest growth in completed qualifications has occurred in the field of education, which experienced an average growth rate of 9.1% over the last four years (to 2000). In particular, there has been a 71% increase in the number of graduates completing a primary teaching qualification since 1997.

The next largest growth has occurred in sport and recreation qualifications (8.9%), and computing qualifications (8.8%).

While the most common field of study was commerce and business (20% of all completions), the number of awards in these fields experienced a moderate 3.2% annual increase.

Student loan scheme debt (June 2001)

Range of loan balances	No. of borrowers	%
$1–$10,000	170 136	54.14
$10,001–20,000	78 800	25.07
$20,001–30,000	34 151	10.86
$30,001–40,000	17 191	5.47
$40,001–50,000	8 166	2.59
$50,001–60,000	3 447	1.10
$60,001–70,000	1 419	0.45
$70,001–80,000	522	0.17
$80,001–90,000	245	0.08
$90,001–100,000	110	0.04
Over $100,001	93	0.03
Total	**314 280**	

- As at 30 June 2001 Inland Revenue has collected $1136 million in loan repayments since the scheme began in 1992.
- The level of overdue loan repayments at 30 June 2001 was just over $53 million.

In 2002 the average student owed $14,000, according to the New Zealand University Students' Association.

Average annual amount borrowed by students

1992	$3 628	1997	$5 494
1993	$3 979	1998	$5 714
1994	$4 309	1999	$4 917
1995	$4 432	2000	$6 222
1996	$4 649		

Notes:
1. The average amount borrowed by students shows a steady increase possibly reflecting increases in student fees.
2. The decrease in average borrowing for 1999 is due to the decrease in the maximum course cost entitlement from $1000 in 1998 to $500 in 1999 and to other changes which encouraged students to use finance from the scheme for purposes related to study.
3. Average borrowing increased again in 2000 when some of the changes made in 1999 were rescinded, and the 'full interest write-off while studying' policy was introduced.

Educating the educators

Teacher training courses are offered by a number of institutions. Courses include:

- Early childhood: three-year initial training courses.
- Primary teacher: usually three years' training followed by two years' teaching.
- Secondary teacher: one-year course for approved graduates; or up to four years for others.
- Special education: speech-language therapy is a four-year degree; other specialised post-graduate courses for other teachers.
- Continuing education: a wide range of professional papers for certified teachers.

Justice and law

The legal system

Hierarchy of courts

- The Judicial Committee of the Privy Council
- The Court of Appeal
- The High Court
- District courts
- Specialist courts
  - Employment Court
  - Family courts
  - Youth courts
  - Maori Land Court and Maori Appellate Court
  - Environment Court
- Tribunals
  - Employment Tribunal
  - Disputes Tribunal
  - Complaints Review Tribunal
  - Residential Tenancies Tribunal
  - Waitangi Tribunal

Sources of law

New Zealand law consists of:

- The common law (case or judge-made law).
- New Zealand statutes made by Parliament.
- United Kingdom statutes passed before 1840 and not since repealed or replaced. Some of constitutional importance remain, such as the Magna Carta of 1297, the Habeas Corpus Act 1679 and the Act of Settlement 1700.
- Subordinate legislation, usually made by local authorities.

The Law Commission is an independent, publicly funded central advisory body for the review, reformation and development of New Zealand law.

Legal aid

- Criminal legal aid is available if the applicant does not seem to have sufficient means to pay for necessary legal representation.
- Civil legal aid is often regarded as a loan, as costs are later recovered.
- Community law centres provide advice to those who cannot afford a lawyer.

Youth justice family group conferences are held to address the offending of young people. Family/whanau members meet with a law enforcement officer and the victims to agree how the offender will be held accountable, and to agree on appropriate intervention plans.

Jury service

In the District Court and High Court the Judge sits alone or with a jury. Various laws say when there has to be a jury, and when there is a choice to have one or not. The Judge decides questions of law, and also directs the jury on the law where necessary.

A jury is made of 12 ordinary people aged between 20 and 65, selected at random from the jury roll, which is based on the electoral roll. Exceptions are if:

- They are involved in justice-related occupations.
- Jury service would cause serious hardship.
- They have recent prison sentences.
- They have been imprisoned for more than three years.

The Crown Law Office provides legal advice and representation to the government. Its main aims are to ensure the government acts lawfully, and that the government is not prevented from lawfully enacting its policies.

Criminal justice

Convictions (distinct cases resulting in conviction, excl. traffic)

	1998	1999	2000
Against the person	12 182	11 563	11 263
Property	19 108	19 216	18 550
Drug	7 313	7 128	6 845
Other	17 010	17 563	16 642

Prison population (annual average inmate numbers)

	1998	1999	2000
Males	5 218	5 429	5 450
Females	232	232	270

*Recorded crime per 10,000 of population by category**

	1999/00	2000/01
Violence	104.7	113.1
Sexual offences	8.2	8.1
Drugs and antisocial	140.2	140.7
Dishonesty	686.3	647.7
Property damage	106.0	105.1
Property abuses	53.6	54.0
Administrative	29.8	33.6
Total	**1 128.6**	**1 102.3**

* Estimated Statistics New Zealand residential population June 2001 quarter, June 2001 provisional.

Over 40% of male prison inmates and over 70% of women inmates have not been imprisoned before.

Corrections system

Community-based sentences

Sentences administered by the community probation service:

- Community service
- Supervision
- Community programme
- Periodic detention (PD)
- Parole
- Home detention

Penal institutions (accommodation maximum and facilities)

Paremoremo (Auck)	611 m	Max/med
Mt Eden (Auck)	471 m 54 f	Max/med/remand
Ohura	100 m	Minimum
Waikeria	895 m	Max/med/min/rem
Tongariro/Rangipo	533 m	Min/corr. training
Wanganui	400 m	Max/med/min/rem
Manawatu	190 m	Med/min/remand
New Plymouth	109 m	Med/min/remand
Hawke's Bay	404 m	Med/min/remand
Rimutaka	446 m	Med/min/remand
Wellington	136 m	Medium
Arohata	107 f	Med/min/rem/corr. train
Addington (Chch)	536 m	Max/med/min
Chch Women's	60 f	Med/min
Rolleston	320 m	Minimum
Dunedin	59 m	Med/min
Invercargill	172 m	Med/min/remand

Note: f = females, m = males.

The new regional prisons programme

The Regional Prisons Programme has been set up by the Department of Justice to help reduce re-offending rates. To help achieve this, facilities will be located close to the home areas of inmates, and will be designed and managed in such a way as to encourage self-discipline and self-responsibility by offenders.

To meet these goals, the Department is building four new regional corrections facilities around New Zealand. They vary in size from 150 cells to 650 cells. Only one (the Auckland Region Women's Corrections Facility) will regularly accommodate maximum-security inmates.

The four facilities are:

- 350-bed men's facility in Northland (to open in late 2003).
- 150-bed women's facility in Manukau City (to open in late 2004).
- 650-bed men's facility near Meremere, south of Auckland (to open in late 2004).
- 330-bed facility in Otago (to open in 2006).

In the 2002/03 government budget, the Department of Corrections will receive a capital contribution of $84.339 million to construct corrections facilities at Rimutaka, Otago, Auckland and Northland, a pilot Day Reporting Centre, and for deferred maintenance and prison security.

International comparisons

The International Centre for Prison Studies (ICPS) has ranked 100 countries with the highest prison population rates, as known to ICPS at June 2002. (This shows prison population per 100,000 of national population: see table next page.)

New Zealand ranks 71st out of the 100 countries, with an imprisonment rate only 22% of that of the USA.

International prison population rates (June 2002)

1.	USA	690
2.	Russian Federation	670
3.	Cayman Islands (UK)	600
10.	Bermuda	447
20.	Latvia	367
30.	Lithuania	303
40.	Tunisia	253
50.	Virgin Islands (UK)	215
60.	Hungary	179
70.	Zimbabwe	163
71.	New Zealand	157
72.	Mexico	156
75.	Colombia	153

New Zealand Police

The New Zealand Police are responsible for enforcing criminal law in New Zealand. Police provide services 24 hours a day, 365 days a year and operate on land, sea and air.

- There are over 400 community-based police stations.
- There are 8800 staff: 7087 were sworn personnel on 30 June 2001; female sworn personnel were 1084 or 15.3% of sworn staff.
- Police respond to more than 1 million emergency (111) calls annually, both genuine and non-genuine (the majority).
- Crime prevention is a key aim.

Key figures for 2000/2001

- Total recorded crime dropped 1.9%.
- 7500 more crimes were solved than the previous year.

- There were 10,500 fewer burglaries than the year before, and more were solved.
- Violent offending increased by 8.6%.
- Provisional traffic results show speed camera infringements increased from 441,408 to 523,362.
- Overall speed offences rose from 124,170 to 176,684, reflecting the detection work of the new Highway Patrol.
- The road toll for the year ended 30 June 2002 was 430, the lowest in nearly four decades.

Recorded and resolved offences

	Recorded	% Variation	Resolved	% Resolved
1991/92	459 196	8.2	136 993	29.8
1992/93	471 035	2.6	155 162	32.9
1993/94	449 982	–4.5	170 369	37.9
1994/95	461 140	2.5	173 675	37.7
1995/96	475 154	3.0	179 826	37.8
1996/97	482 831	1.6	178 140	36.9
1997/98	465 834	–3.5	177 687	38.1
1998/99	455 552	–2.2	174 576	38.3
1999/00	432 354	–5.1	174 611	40.4
2000/01	424 286	–1.9	182 137	42.9

Note: These are reports of offences, not all of which resulted in court convictions.

Of convictions (other than traffic offences) in 1998, 84% involved male offenders and 16% female. Where ethnicity was known 46% of cases involved Europeans, 44% were Maori, 8% Pacific Islands people and 2% others. Teenagers were involved in 21% of cases, and a total of 64% of offenders were under 30 years of age.

Police operations

- Armed offenders squads
- Special tactics groups
- Search and rescue
- Youth education service
- Police dogs
- Community constables
- Youth aid section
- Neighbourhood support groups
- National drug intelligence bureau
- Police infringement bureau

In the year to June 2001, there were 1997 assaults on police.

Capital punishment

History of capital punishment

1840	New Zealand inherited state capital punishment with other British law.
1862	Hanging no longer in public.
1941	Death sentence for murder abolished, still applied for treason and piracy.
1950	Death sentence for murder reinstated.
1958	Death sentence for murder suspended.
1961	Death sentence for murder and piracy abolished.
1989	Abolition of the death penalty removed sentence for treason.

Executions

- 1842 first hanging of man found guilty of murder.
- Information about hangings sketchy until 1880.
- 36 hanged between 1880 and 1941.
- Eight hanged between 1951 and 1957.
- The only woman hanged was Minnie Dean in 1895.

Creation and recreation

Statutory holidays

New Year's Day	1 January
New Year's Holiday	2 January
Waitangi (NZ) Day	6 February
Good Friday	Moveable feast
Easter Monday	Moveable feast
Anzac Day	25 April
Queen's Birthday (observed)	3 June
Labour Day	4th Monday in October
Christmas Day	25 December
Boxing Day	26 December

Anniversary Days

(Observed on working days if fall on weekends.)

Wellington	22 January
Auckland and Northland	29 January
Nelson and Buller	1 February
Taranaki	31 March
Otago	23 March
Southland	17 January
South Canterbury	25 September
Hawke's Bay	1 November
Marlborough	1 November
Canterbury	16 December
Chatham Islands	30 November
Westland	1 December

- Most workers are also entitled to sick, bereavement and three week's annual leave. In 2002 paid parental leave was introduced.
- Labour Day in New Zealand commemorates the introduction of the eight-hour working day, first instigated by the carpenter Samuel Parnell at Petone in 1840. The first Labour Day was celebrated throughout the country in 1890.

Arts and culture

New Zealanders report a high level of participation in broadly defined arts and cultural activities. In 1998, 93% of the adult population took part in cultural and arts activities. The following can only be a rough outline of creative activities in this country.

Some famous creative New Zealanders

Frances Hodgkins	artist
Charles Goldie	artist
Katherine Mansfield	author
Len Lye	filmmaker and kinetic sculptor
Keith Murray	ceramic artist
Kiri Te Kanawa	singer
Jon Trimmer	ballet dancer
Jane Campion	film-maker
Colin McCahon	artist
Janet Frame	author
Sam Neill	actor
Keri Hulme	author
Allen Curnow	poet

Margaret Mahy	children's author
Tim and Neil Finn	singer songwriters
Elizabeth Knox	author
Peter Jackson	film-maker
Fran Walsh	screen writer

Maori arts

Historically, Maori did not separate their creations into art, artefacts or culture. Taonga, now admired as art, were originally created for practical purposes but were also associated with the terms mana (prestige), tapu (highly valued and restricted) and whakapapa (genealogy).

Traditional Maori arts include:

- whakairo (wood carving)
- kowhaiwhai (rafter patterns)
- raranga (weaving)
- tukutuku (lattice work)
- ta moko (tattooing)
- waiata (songs and chants)
- haka (dance)
- taonga puoro (traditional musical instruments)
- karanga (traditional call of welcome)
- whaikorero (oratory)
- mau rakau (the art of weaponry)

Traditional artforms are still being created and preserved, but contemporary Maori artists are also developing innovative new techniques within the styles handed down through the generations, and exploring modern mediums.

The huge growth in the numbers joining kapa haka performance clubs is an example of the cultural renaissance of the past 25 years.

The Aotearoa Traditional Maori Performing Arts Festival was first held in Rotorua in 1972. This bi-annual festival brings together kapa haka clubs from all over the country in competition and celebration.

Pacific arts

Pacific peoples have made great contributions to New Zealand and world arts. Examples are:

- Jonathan Lemalu, a young Samoan singer from Dunedin, winner of many awards, including the presitigious Eisteddfod's International Singer competition in Wales.
- Auckland-based, Tongan-born steel guitarist Bill Sevesi, composer of over 200 songs, and honoured in the Steel Guitar Hall of Fame in St Louis Missouri.
- Novelist and professor Albert Wendt and poet and novelist Alistair Te Ariki Campbell. These authors have contributed greatly to New Zealand's literature and also to the establishment and growth of a wider Pacific literature.
- Samoan-born painter and sculptor Fatu Feu'u, winner of many awards, and appointed residencies at two art schools. He is considered the inaugurator of modern Pacific art and sculpture in New Zealand.

The Pasifika festival, held annually in Auckland, is a celebration of Pacific Island and Maori food, art, dance, and other cultural activities. Over 100,000 people attend the event.

Art galleries and museums

New Zealand has about 600 public museums and art galleries. (See: www. nzmuseums.co.nz. for a list of New Zealand museums.) The Museum of New Zealand Te Papa Tongarewa in Wellington opened in 1998. It contains over 20 major constructed exhibitions.

National performing arts organisations

- New Zealand Symphony Orchestra
- New Zealand Chamber Orchestra
- National Youth Orchestra
- Royal New Zealand Ballet
- New Zealand School of Dance
- Chamber Music New Zealand
- New Zealand Choral Foundation
- Aotearoa Traditional Maori Performing Arts Society
- New Zealand Film Commission

The New Zealand Festival is held biannually in Wellington. It began in 1984, and is now the country's largest arts festival, attracting artists from all over the world, and presenting many new New Zealand works. The next one will be in 2004.

*Top 10 songs of the last 75 years**

1. 'Nature' (1969), *Wayne Mason – Fourmyula.*
2. 'Don't Dream It's Over' (1986) *Neil Finn – Crowded House.*
3. 'Loyal' (1987) *Dave Dobbyn.*
4. 'Counting The Beat' (1981) *Phil Judd, Mark Hough, Wayne Stevens – The Swingers.*
5. 'Six Months In A Leaky Boat' (1982) *Tim Finn – Split Enz.*
6. 'Sway' (1997) *Bic Runga.*
7. 'Slice Of Heaven' (1986) *Dave Dobbyn.*
8. 'Victoria' (1982) *Jordan Luck – Dance Exponents.*
9. 'She Speeds' (1987) *Shayne Carter – Straitjacket Fits.*
10. 'April Sun In Cuba' (1978) *Paul Hewson, Mark Hunter – Dragon.*

*Chosen in October 2001, by the members of the Australasian Performing Rights Association (APRA) and an academy of 100, who were invited to vote for the best and most significant songs of the last 75 years.

Reading and writing

New Zealanders are enthusiastic readers, spending on average 44 minutes a day reading.

Newspapers and magazines

New Zealand has:

- 25 daily newspapers.
- 2 Sunday newspapers.
- 120 community newspapers.
- 4700 magazines readily available, 700 of which are published here.

See the National Library (http://tepuna.natlib.govt.nz/web_directory/NZ/serials.htm) for a list of New Zealand journals, magazines and newspapers.

> New Zealand rates highly in international comparisons of press freedom, and has done for many years. (See www.freedomhouse.org.)

Book awards

The premier adult book awards in New Zealand are the Montana New Zealand Book Awards.

Montana New Zealand book award winners since 1998

2002

- Deutz Medal for Fiction: Marriner, C. *Stonedogs.*
- Montana Medal for Non Fiction: Hood, L. *A City Possessed: The Christchurch Civic Creche Case.*

2001

- Deutz Medal for Fiction: Jones, L. *The Book of Fame.*
- Montana Medal for Non-Fiction: King, M. *Wrestling with the Angel: A life of Janet Frame.*

2000

- Deutz Medal for Fiction: Marshall, O. *Harlequin Rex.*

- Montana Medal for Non-Fiction: Sydney, G. *The Art of Grahame Sydney.*

1999

- Deutz Medal for Fiction: Knox, E. *The Vintner's Luck.*
- Montana Medal for Non-Fiction: Nicholson, H. *The Loving Stitch: A history of knitting and spinning in New Zealand.*

1998

- Deutz Medal for Fiction: Gee, M. *Live Bodies.*
- Montana Medal for Non-Fiction: Orsman, H. *Dictionary of New Zealand English.*

In 2002 thirty-three collections of poetry were submitted (including many by this country's finest poets) to the Montana Book Awards.

Children's books

New Zealand has many very successful children's authors, illustrators and publishers. Several authors have received international acclaim and local publishers export reading series to numerous countries. The New Zealand Post Children's Book Festival is a popular industry promotion.

Margaret Mahy Award

This is awarded for distinguished services to children's literature, literacy or publishing.

1991	Margaret Mahy	1997	Ann Mallinson
1992	Dorothy Butler	1998	William Taylor
1993	Joy Cowley	1999	Lynley Dodd
1994	Betty Gilderdale	2000	Gavin Bishop
1995	Elsie Locke	2001	Sherryl Jordan
1996	Tessa Duder	2002	Maurice Gee

Libraries

Local libraries are funded by local councils. For information about library services contact the council concerned. For a listing of councils see: www.localgovt.co.nz.

Te Puna Matauranga, the National Library, is a national organisation. It has regional centres in Auckland, Palmerston North and Christchurch, and district centres around the country. Most of its collections, services and facilities are in the head office in Wellington. (See: www.natlib.govt.nz/flash.html)

Film and video

Local films in New Zealand: box-office successes

1.	*Lord of the Rings: The Fellowship of the Ring*, Peter Jackson (2002)
2.	*Once Were Warriors*,* Lee Tamahori (1994)
3.	*The Piano*, Jane Campion (1992)
4.	*What Becomes Of The Broken Hearted?*,* Ian Mune (1998)
5.	*Footrot Flats*, Murray Ball (1986)
6.	*Goodbye Pork Pie*,* Geoff Murphy (1981)
7.	*The Frighteners*, Peter Jackson (1996)
8.	*Scarfies*,* Robert Sarkies (1997)
9.	*Came A Hot Friday*,* Ian Mune (1985)
10.	*Heavenly Creatures*,* Peter Jackson (1994)

*Movies in which the New Zealand Film Commission has invested.

- Sam Neil, a New Zealand actor perhaps best known for his work in the *Jurassic Park* films, has also won or been nominated for 13 awards, including several Golden Globe nominations, and was given the Order of the British Empire for 'services to acting'.

- The first recorded performance of a play was Christmas 1841. The first true theatre was the Royal Victoria in Wellington, which opened in 1843.

Oscar winners

Lord of the Rings: The Fellowship of the Ring received the most nominations for Oscars in 2001, and received four wins:

- Original score – Howard Shore
- Cinematography – Andrew Lesnie
- Makeup
- Visual effects

The Lord of the Rings became the ninth film ever to receive 13 Oscar nominations or more. Two other films in Academy Awards history have had 14 nominations, and six other films have had 13 nominations.

- New Zealand-born Russell Crowe was nominated for the third consecutive year in 2002 for best actor in a leading role for *A Beautiful Mind.* He won best actor in the 2001 Academy Awards.
- New Zealander Jane Campion was the first (and only) woman director of a Best Picture nominee (*The Piano*, 1993 Academy Awards) and recipient of a Best Director nomination. She won an Oscar for the best original screenplay.
- New Zealander Anna Paquin was the second youngest Oscar winner (at 11) for best supporting actress in *The Piano.*

In 1994–95 more New Zealanders went to see *Once Were Warriors* than any other film from any other source at that time. This record was surpassed by *The Lord of the Rings: The Fellowship of the Ring* in 2002.

Economic effects of The Lord of the Rings

A scoping study done for the New Zealand Film Commission, April 2002, found that some of the immediate effects of *The Lord of the Rings* trilogy being filmed in New Zealand were:

- $352.7 million expenditure by the production company in New Zealand (to March 2002). The above New Zealand expenditure includes:
  - labour costs of $187.7 million.
  - digital effects costs of $99 million.
  - miniatures and creature costs of $36.5 million.
  - location costs of $31.3 million.
  - construction costs of $25.1 million.
  - transportation costs of $12 million.
- This level of expenditure produced peak period employment of around 1500 people per week (excluding any day labour or extras).
- It is about 3200 person years employment of New Zealand tax residents for the four years from 1997 to 2001.
- Around 5000 vendors were used, most of them in New Zealand.
- Expenditure will continue as the next two films are prepared for release.

Television

- The first public television broadcast was on 1 June 1960. There were 4000 television sets in 1961; and 500,000 by 1964.
- Colour television was introduced in 1974.
- The second television station, also state-owned, started in 1975.
- The first privately owned television station, TV3, began in 1989.
- Private stations now include TV3, TV4, Prime, Sky, Saturn

as well as regional and special interest channels.

- Watching television is the favourite pastime of most New Zealanders. In 1998/89, people aged 12 years and over spent on average three hours and eight minutes a day watching 'the box'.
- About 98% of New Zealand households have television (96% have telephones).

Local content

- Local content on New Zealand television accounts for a much smaller proportion of total transmission time than in Australia, Canada, Ireland or Norway.
- News and Current Affairs is the single largest local content genre, comprising 33% of total local hours. This was an increase in 2001 of 3% on 2000 (see table below).

Total hours by genre (1999–2001)

	1999	2000	2001
Drama/Comedy	364	386	363
Sports	1 010	1 239	791
News/Current affairs	1 835	1 876	2 073
Entertainment	496	433	532
Children's	620	591	488
Children's drama	9	6	15
Maori	287	371	396
Documentaries	331	242	260
Information	1 191	1 041	1 272
Total NZ content	**6 143**	**6 185**	**6 190**
% of schedule	**23.4%**	**23.5%**	**23.6%**

Notes: 1. These hours are for TV One, TV2 and TV3 only (TV3 commenced in Nov. 1989). 2. Figures have been rounded.

Natural History New Zealand Ltd is a television production company based in Dunedin, and is 100% owned by Fox Television Studios. It is one of the world's largest producers of wildlife documentaries, and also produces adventure, travel and science documentaries. These have earned the company more than 150 international awards.

New Zealand radio

There are both state-owned and commercial radio stations.

State-owned radio

Radio New Zealand Limited is a Crown entity. It has:

- three non-commercial radio networks: National Radio (mainly news and information); Concert FM (fine music); the AM network (broadcasts Parliament).
- Radio New Zealand International, a short-wave service.
- Radio New Zealand News and Current Affairs.
- Sound Archives/Nga Taonga Korero.

Live sports broadcasting began with a rugby commentary in 1926, from Lancaster Park in Christchurch, followed by commentaries on cricket, boxing and hockey.

Private radio

The Ministry of Economic Development estimated there were 190 private radio stations in 2001, compared with 64 in 1988.

The oldest radio station in the Commonwealth started in Dunedin in 1922, and is still broadcasting as station 4XD.

Sports and fitness

Many New Zealanders love sports and the outdoors. This love has produced numerous world-class sportspeople, in many fields, only a few of which are listed here.

A few famous sportspeople

The 1905–06 Originals	First All Blacks rugby team
Anthony Wilding	Wimbledon champion 1910–13
George Nepia	Great All Black fullback, 1924–30
Jack Lovelock	Runner, winner of classic 1500 m, 1936 Olympics
Bert Sutcliffe	Cricketer, record-breaking batsman of 1940s and 50s
Edmund Hillary	Conqueror of Mount Everest, 1953
Yvette Williams	Olympic gold-medallist athlete of the 1950s
Bob Charles	World-class golfer from 1950s to present
Philippa Gould	World record setting swimmer of 1950s
Colin Meads	All Black rugby player 1957–91
Murray Halberg	First New Zealander to run sub-four-minute mile
Arthur Lydiard	Coach of middle-distance running Olympic winners
Peter Snell	Record-breaking middle distance runner of 1960s
Eve Rimmer	Gold winner in many Paralympic events, 1968–80
NZ Rowing Eight	Dominated world rowing in early 1970s
Richard Hadlee	Fast bowling cricketer, 1970s to 1990
John Walker	Broke the 3 min 50 sec mile in 1975
Ivan Mauger	World speedway champion of 1970s
Ian Ferguson	Canoeist, winner of three golds in 1984 Olympics
Susan Devoy	World champion squash player 1984–92
Mark Todd	Horseman 1980s to present

Peter Blake	Yachtsman, leader of Team New Zealand's America's Cup win in 1995
Danyon Loader	Double gold medal winner for swimming, 1996 Olympics
Erin Baker	Triathlete 1980s–1990s; several world championship wins
Jonah Lomu	All Black rugby player 1990s to present

School and club sports

- Almost three-quarters of boys and girls are involved in sport and active leisure at school.
- Almost a quarter also take part in sports and activities organised by the school before or after the main school day.
- Around a third of young people play sport with a club, although this is more common for boys than girls.

Top five sports/activities played with clubs (5–17 year olds)

Boys	Girls
Soccer (17%)	Swimming (17%)
Rugby union (16%)	Netball (13%)
Swimming (14%)	Horse riding (10%)
Cricket (8%)	Tennis (8%)
Hockey (8%)	Soccer (6%)

Note: The figures show the percentage of young club members who participate in each sport, e.g. 17% of boys who are club members play soccer, the figure for all boys is around 6%.

Young Maori spend most time in active leisure and sports – on average over 6.5 hours/week. Young people from both a Maori and European background spend more time being active than young people from other cultures.

Top 15 sports for adults (1998)

Men

1. Golf	26%	332 500
2. Cricket	15%	184 000
3. Tennis	14%	181 500
4. Touch football	14%	173 900
5. Rugby union	11%	137 100
6. Motor sports	10%	124 400
7. Shooting	9%	115 500
8. Basketball	9%	109 100
9. Yachting	7%	92 600
10. Skiing	7%	91 400
11. Squash	7%	90 100
12. Soccer	7%	83 800
13. Bowls (lawn)	6%	71 100
14. Cricket (indoors)	5%	66 000
15. Volleyball	5%	66 000

Women

1. Netball	11%	154 900
2. Tennis	10%	131 800
3. Golf	9%	127 700
4. Touch football	7%	88 300
5. Skiing	7%	88 300
6. Horse riding	6%	82 900
7. Basketball	5%	61 100
8. Badminton	4%	59 800
9. Bowls (indoor)	4%	58 400

10. Yachting	4%	55 700
11. Cricket	4%	53 000
12. Volleyball	4%	50 300
13. Bowls (lawn)	4%	47 500
14. Squash	3%	34 000
15. Motor sports	2%	31 200

Notes: 1. Figures rounded. 2. Motor sports includes motor cycling, trail biking and motor racing.

Coronary heart disease, colon cancer and diabetes caused around a third (just over 7800) of the adult deaths in 1994. Around a fifth of these deaths can be attributed to physical inactivity.

Most popular sports/active leisure for women

1. Walking	8. Fishing
2. Gardening	9. Cycling
3. Swimming	10. Netball
4. Exercising at home	11. Tennis
6. Exercise classes/gym	12. Golf
7. Aerobics	13. Tramping

Approximately two out of every three adults report spending 2.5 hours or more each week participating in leisure-time physical activity that is as intense as brisk walking. The proportion of physically active adults has been estimated as 66% by the 1996/97 Hillary Commission Physical Activity Survey, and at 61% by the 1996/97 New Zealand Health Survey. Sports and physical activities are more popular with men than women, and young people are more active than older adults.

Most popular sports/active leisure for men

1.	Walking	8.	Exercise classes/gym
2.	Gardening	9.	Running
3.	Fishing	10.	Cycling
4.	Swimming	11.	Tennis
6.	Golf	12.	Touch football
7.	Exercising at home	13.	Tramping

The most commonly performed haka by rugby teams and schools is one said to be composed by Te Rauparaha (upon being hidden from his pursuers in a kumara pit by the hairy-legged Te Wharerangi, who sat over the entrance). A standard version is:

Ka mate! Ka mate!	It is death! It is death!
Ka ora! Ka ora!	It is life! It is life!
Tenei te tangata puhuruhuru	This is the hairy person
Nana nei i tiki mai	Who caused the sun to shine
I whakawhiti re ra!	
Upane! Upane!	Abreast! Keep abreast!
Upane! Ka upane!	The rank! Hold fast!
Whiti te ra!	Into the sun that shines!

Sports injuries: number of ACC claims

	1998/99	1999/00	2000/01
Netball	1 561	1 309	1 437
Other	1 143	914	919
Rugby Union	5 410	4 852	5 042
Soccer	1 507	1 397	1 447
Swimming	1 433	811	956

Olympics

The first modern Olympics were held in Athens in 1896. New Zealand competed as part of the Australasian team in 1908, gaining a bronze medal. New Zealand's first gold medal was for swimming in 1912.

New Zealand sent its first official Olympic team to the 7th Olympiad in Antwerp, Belgium, in 1920.

Summer Olympic medals won (1908 to 2000)

Gold	31
Silver	13
Bronze	32
Total	**76**

Note: These are per event, not person.

New Zealand has one medal winner in the Winter Olympic Games. Slalom skier Annelise Coberger won silver in the 1992 Games.

New Zealand's biggest haul of 16 gold medals was for eight different events in the 1984 Los Angeles games.

Recent gold medal winners

- **1984, Los Angeles:** I. Ferguson (canoeing K1 500 m, K2 500 m, K4 1000 m); P. MacDonald (canoeing K2 500 m, K4 1000 m); A. Thompson (canoeing K1 1000 m, K4 1000 m); G. Bramwell (canoeing, K4 1000 m); M. Todd (equestrian, three-day event); R. Coutts (Finn class yatching); R. Sellers, C. Timms (Tornado class yachting); C. Robertson, S. OBrien, K. Trask and L. O'Connell (rowing, coxless four).
- **1988, Seoul:** M. Todd (equestrian, three-day event); B. Kendall (board sailing); I. Ferguson, P. MacDonald (canoeing K2 500 m).

- **1992, Barcelona:** B. Kendall (board sailing).
- **1996, Atlanta:** D. Loader (swimming, 200 m and 400 m freestyle); B. Tait (equestrian three-day event).
- **2000, Sydney:** R. Waddell (rowing, single sculls).

The Paralympics

Paralympics New Zealand is the recognised National Sporting Organisation for people with disabilities. (See www.paralympicsnz.org.nz)

Important dates in sports for people with disabilities

1962	New Zealand sends Pompey Heremaia of Auckland to the Perth Commonwealth Paraplegic Games.
1968	First national games in Auckland.
1968	Fifteen athletes to the third Paralympics in Tel Aviv.
1980	Eve Rimmer retires with one bronze, six silver, eight gold medals.
1996	Paralymics: team of 33 athletes finish 19th of 102 countries.
2000	Paralympics: team of 70 athletes attend, winning six gold, eight silver and four bronze medals.

The Commonwealth Games

The first Commonwealth Games were held in 1930, in Hamilton, Canada. There were 400 participants. The Games had a forerunner in the Festival of Empire in 1911, in London.

Games held in New Zealand and number of participants

1950	Auckland	590
1974	Christchurch	1 276
1990	Auckland	2 100

Commonwealth Games medals won (1930–2002)

Gold	118
Silver	155
Bronze	221
Total	**494**

Note: These are per event, not person.

The 1990 Auckland Commonwealth Games were the most successful for New Zealand athletes. They gained 17 gold, 14 silver and 27 bronze medals (58 total). The second most successful were the 1950 Empire Games in Auckland, with 52 medals. The third most successful were the 2002 Manchester Games where New Zealand finished fifth on the medal table with 11 gold, 13 silver and 21 bronze medals (total 45).

Recent Commonwealth Games medals (gold, silver, bronze)

1962	Perth	10	12	10
1966	Kingston	8	5	13
1970	Edinburgh	2	6	6
1974	Christchurch	9	8	18
1978	Edmonton	5	6	8
1982	Brisbane	5	8	13
1986	Edinburgh	8	16	14
1990	Auckland	17	14	27
1994	Victoria	5	13	11
1998	Kuala Lumpur	8	6	20
2002	Manchester	11	13	21

Popular outdoor leisure activities

- Cycling: mountain biking is particularly popular.
- Fishing: in lakes and rivers (mostly trout and salmon) and sea (surfcasting, netting, kite fishing, wharf fishing, rock fishing, line fishing, big-game fishing).
- Mountaineering, tramping: many short and longer walks.
- Shooting and hunting: game bird season starts first weekend in May, last six to eight weeks. Few restrictions on big game (mostly deer, pigs).
- Skiing, snowboarding: June to late October in both islands.
- Surfing: many good beaches in both islands.
- Windsurfing: and any other opportunities to get on in or near water.

- New Zealand first won the America's Cup, yachting's major international trophy, in 1995. In 2000 it successfully defended the cup when Team New Zealand beat Prada, the Italian challenger. The next challenge is in Auckland in 2003.
- New Zealand's pastoral base and pioneering background are shown in the popularity of such events as sheepshearing and wood-chopping competitions.

Gaming and betting

Gaming and betting have long been part of New Zealand culture, but for most of the 20th century the only legal outlets were the Totaliser Agency Board (TAB), lotteries and housie. That changed from 1987 onwards, when Lotto was introduced, followed by the legalising of gaming machines and then casinos.

New Zealand has a very strong horsebreeding sector, the legacy of years of racing. Export of thoroughbred horses is worth about $100 million per year.

Gaming opportunities

Gaming opportunities include:

- Six casinos offering around 15 different types of table games, plus gaming machines with video poker, video keno and spinning reel games.
- Lotto, Lotto Strike, Powerball, TeleBingo, Daily Keno and Instant Kiwi (all offered by the Lotteries Commission) at more than 900 terminals.
- Race and sports betting through almost 500 TAB outlets.
- Some 17,700 licensed non-casino gaming machines operated at around 2100 different (mainly pub and club) sites around the country (December 2001).
- Smaller local forms of gambling, such as lotteries/raffles, housie and prize competitions.
- Overseas gambling by Internet.

Casinos

Five casinos are currently operating in New Zealand:

- Sky City (Auckland)
- Christchurch
- Dunedin

- Sky Alpine (Queenstown)
- Steamer Wharf (Queenstown)
- Riverside Casino (Hamilton).

The ability to seek a premises licence for a new casino has been temporarily suspended until 16 October 2003 by a statutory moratorium that started in October 1997.

The expenditure on casino gambling (turnover minus prizes) for year ended 30 June 2001 was $369 million.

The number of machines and games in casinos (January 2002) was:

Table games	169
Gaming machines	2 240

Gaming participation

Five-yearly research by the Department of Internal Affairs suggests that in any year 85–90% of the adult population participate at least once in some gaming. This percentage has been stable over the last 15 years.

The National Gambling Prevalence Survey (1999) found:

- Some 41% of those aged 18 and over participated in gaming at least weekly.
- Over a third of the adult population played Lotto on a weekly basis.
- Very few adults participated regularly (i.e. at least weekly) in any single form of gaming other than Lotto.

Gaming expenditure

In 2000 the main components of gaming expenditure were:

- $450 million on non-casino gaming machines.
- $343 million in casinos (on table games and casino gaming machines).

- $277 million on Lotteries Commission products.
- $227 million on race and sports betting.

Since 1988 almost all gaming growth has been in casinos and gaming machines. Race and sports betting have been relatively static, while over the last two years the amount spent on Lotteries Commission products has declined.

The National Prevalence Survey (1999) reported that adults who gambled on at least one form of gaming in the six months before being surveyed spent an average of $41 a month. A selection of other findings of interest were:

- Men typically spent $53 per month compared with women, who spent $30.
- People aged 45–54 were the highest spending of the age groups, at $58 per month.
- Pacific Island people ($62 per month) and Maori ($49 per month) were the highest spending ethnic groups. Europeans and Asians were next at $40 per month and $38 per month respectively.
- People with degrees or higher qualifications were the lowest spenders.

Prevalence of problem gambling

Based on a study of 6452 people in 1999, social science researchers Abbott and Volberg estimated that 58,000 to 107,700 (2.1% to 3.9%) of New Zealanders aged 18 and over have had a gambling problem at some time in their lives. This figure is almost certainly conservative, for a variety of reasons.

Statistics on new problem gambling personal counselling clients in 2000 show the primary source of their problems are:

- Non-casino gaming machines, 68.4% of clients.
- Casino gaming machines, 12.5%.
- Race betting, 10.6%.

SECTION 3

Resources and economy

Resources

Water

Total estimated water resources are 300,000 million cubic metres. Annual distribution varies widely throughout the country.

Water consumption (million cu m) per year

Hydroelectric generation (reusable)	100 000
Irrigation	1 100
Livestock	350
Industry	260
Households	210

Approximately 87% of the population have a public water supply. The remainder have their own domestic supply, such as from rainwater collection or an aquifer bore.

Water quality

The quality of New Zealand drinking water is generally high. Agriculture, urbanisation and industry pose most threats to water quality.

Soil

New Zealand Soil Classification

There are 15 New Zealand Soil Classification soil orders. The most common soil order is 'brown soils'. This type of soil has moderate to low fertility. However, there is a huge range of soil variations and microclimates.

Topoclimate mapping is the combined mapping of the soils and climate of an area at the same time and scale, enabling growers to work out the best use of their land. Topoclimate South (www.topoclimate-south.co.nz) has been carrying out detailed topoclimate mapping in Southland, and Topoclimate Services Pty Ltd (www.topoclimate.com) is promoting this uniquely New Zealand concept worldwide.

Energy resources

Energy contributes about 3% to New Zealand's gross domestic product (GDP) and directly employs around 8000 people or 0.5% of the workforce.

Energy flows through the New Zealand economy from supply to end use, with some energy being transformed from one type to another (such as from coal to electricity). Some energy is lost in transformation and transportation, so more primary energy is supplied than the consumer uses.

- New Zealand's total primary energy supply for the calendar year 2000 was down 1.9% from 758 pentajoules (PJ) from 774 PJ in 1999.
- Total consumer energy for 2000 increased 3.3% to 460 PJ from 445 PJ in 1999. Most of this was used for domestic transport, which made up 41% of total consumer energy (188 PJ).

Primary energy sources

- Imported oil and oil products.
- Indigenous oil and gas (mostly offshore and onshore in Taranaki).
- Hydroelectric (North and South Islands).
- Geothermal electricity (central North Island).
- Coal (Southland, West Coast, Huntly).

Total primary energy supply for calendar year (PJ)

1998	703
1999	775
2000	758

Primary energy supply sources 2000 (PJ)

Oil (total imported and indigenous)	250
Gas	235
Hydro	88
Geothermal	86
Other renewables	52
Coal	47

For the calendar year 2000, fossil fuels contributed 70% (532 PJ) of the total primary energy supplies, and renewables contributed 30% (226 PJ).

Energy transformation

New Zealand's energy transformation industry includes petroleum refining, petrochemicals and electricity generation.

Overall, energy transformation in 2000 was around 18% lower than the 1999 level. This was mainly due to a decrease in electricity generation from geothermal and coal sources.

Consumer energy

Total consumer energy fuel shares from 1974 and 2000

Oil	55%	48%
Electricity	21%	27%
Gas	3.3%	8.5%
Coal	15%	7.6%

Geothermal direct use increased slightly from 2.5% in 1980 to 3% in 2000, while other renewables stayed steady at about 5%.

Total consumer energy for calendar year (PJ)

1997	429.3
1998	439.0
1999	445.2
2000	460.0

Consumer energy consumption 2000 (PJ)

Oil (total imported and indigenous)	220.0
Electricity	122.4
Gas	39.1
Coal	35.1
Other renewables (e.g. biogas, wastes, wood)	29.6
Geothermal direct use	13.8

Total consumer energy by sector 2000 (PJ and percentage)

Domestic transport	188.3	40.9%
Industrial	149.0	32.4%
Residential	59.8	13.0%
Commercial (excl. co-generation)	43.7	9.5%
Agriculture	19.2	4.2%

- New Zealand is self-sufficient in all energy forms except oil.
- Energy contributes about 3% to New Zealand's GDP, and directly employs around 8000 people.

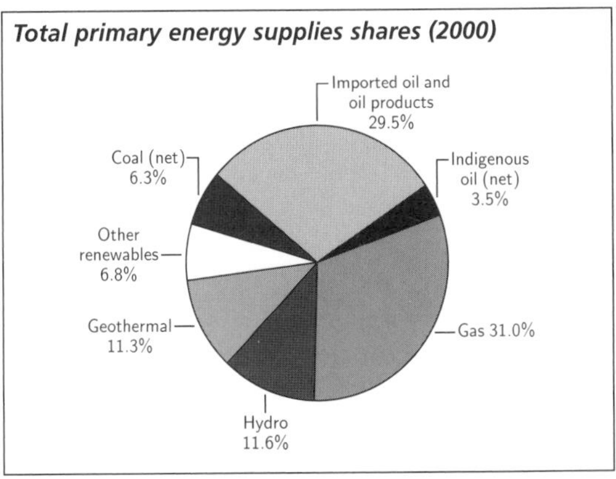

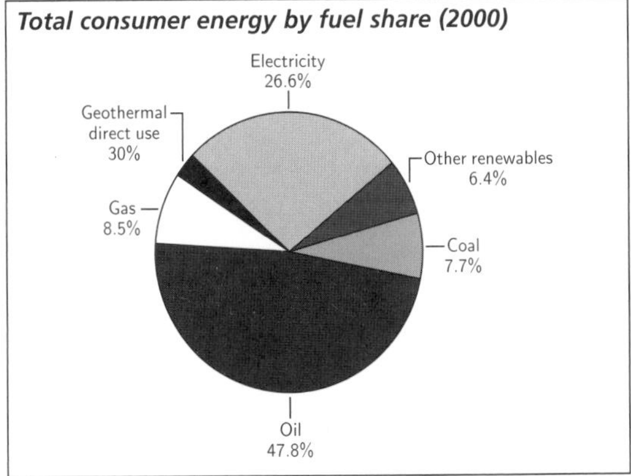

Note: 'Other renewables' includes electricity generation from wind, biogas, industrial waste and wood. Source: Statistics New Zealand.

Oil

- New Zealand-produced oil comes from onshore and offshore oil fields in the Taranaki region. About 75% comes from the offshore Maui field.
- As at 1 July 2001 the remaining oil reserves were estimated at 89.7 million barrels. 63% of this total reserve is part of the Maui field.
- Average daily production of crude oil and condensate is about 53,000 barrels, or 8.5 million litres.
- About 20% of local production goes to the only oil refinery, at Marsden Point, near Whangarei. The rest is exported.
- New Zealand imports crude oil and refined petroleum from Saudi Arabia, Australia, the United Arab Emirates, Malaysia and Indonesia.
- For the year ending September 2001 New Zealand's production of crude oil, condensate and naptha was relatively unchanged from the preceding year, and the country's self-sufficiency in oil at 34% was relatively unchanged.

Vehicle fuel use (year ending September 2001)

- Overall petrol consumption fell by less than 1%.
- Premium unleaded petrol consumption declined by 9%, but this was largely offset by a 2% increase in consumption of regular unleaded petrol.
- Consumption of diesel increased by 2%.
- Consumption of LPG increased by 17%.

Leaded petrol sale has been banned since 1 October 1999.

Electricity generation

- The first public electricity supply was established at Reefton in 1888. Hydro was the sole source of electricity until 1958 when the coal-burning Meremere station was opened, and the Wairakei geothermal scheme began.

- Over two-thirds of hydroelectricity is generated in the South Island, and all geothermal electricity is generated in the North Island.
- Total electricity generation for the September year 2001 at 38,690 gigawatt hours was about 2.7% higher than for September year 2000.

There have been major changes in the way electricity is distributed and sold in New Zealand. For a list of webpages dealing with these changes see *Chronology of New Zealand Electricity Reform* on www.med.govt.nz/ers/electric/chronology/index.html.

Gas

As at 1 July 2001, the total remaining gas reserves are estimated at 155 billion cubic metres. Some 55% of this is within the Maui field.

New Zealand gas production in the year to September 2001 rose by 6%, with 78% coming from the Maui field.

Gas usage (year ending September 2001)

- About 37% was used for petrochemical production.
- 47% for electricity generation. The gas use for electricity generation (including co-generation) was 24% higher than in the previous year. The cold, dry winter of 2001 meant more gas generation was needed as there was less water available for hydro generation.
- 16% for industrial, commercial and domestic purposes.

Coal

Coal occurs widely in New Zealand. Total resources are estimated at about 15 billion tonnes, of which 8.6 billion tonnes are judged economically retrievable. Most of this is in the South Island.

Coal usage (year ending September 2001)

- Coal production in the year was 4.1 million tonnes, an increase of 12% on the previous year.
- Coal exports grew by 240 kilotonnes, a 16% increase.

Renewable sources

- Hydroelectricity
- Geothermal electricity
- Wood for heating
- Geothermal for heating
- Landfill gas
- Solar
- Wind

Total renewable consumer energy was 135 PJ for the calendar year 2000. This was an increase of 7.7% over three years.

Renewable consumer energy 2000 (percentage and PJ)

Renewable electricity	67.8%	91.3 PJ
Other renewables (incl biogas, wood, industrial waste)	21.9%	29.6 PJ
Geothermal direct use	10.3%	13.8 PJ

Mineral resources (non-petroleum minerals)

New Zealand contains a wide variety of minerals as a result of its diverse geology and tectonic history.

In terms of volume extracted and/or value, coal, gold and ironsand are the most significant minerals. There is also extraction of silver, aggregate, limestone, clay, dolomite, pumice, salt, serpentine, silica, sulphur, zeolite and bentonite.

In addition, there are potential or established deposits of titanium (ilmenite beachsands), platinum and phosphate as well as many other non-metallic minerals.

Gold

Gold is found:

- As lode gold in quartz veins.
- Finely disseminated through host rocks.
- In river gravels.

The offically recorded gold production to 1995 was 958 tonnes, worth approximately $20 billion at July 2002 prices. The total production would have been considerably higher than what was recorded, as much was not declared to authorities.

Gold production increased 11% from 1998 to 1999 to reach a total of 8.6 tonnes. Most gold came from the hardrock mines of Macraes (Otago) and Martha Mine (Waihi).

Silver

Silver almost always occurs with gold. The Coromandel mines have produced the most silver to date. Twenty-four tonnes were mined in 1999.

Iron

There are large resources of iron ore in the black sand beaches on the South Island's West Coast and from Wanganui to Muriwai in the North Island. Two deposits are currently mined:

- At Waikato North Head titanomagnetite slurry is smelted with scrap to produce steel products at the Glenbrook steel mill.
- Concentrate slurry from Taharoa, on the coast south of Kawhia Harbour, is exported to Japan, South Korea and China.

Non-metallic minerals

- **Aggregates:** The products of a variety of rocks, gravel and sand, used for construction and in concrete; found throughout the country.

- **Clays:** Many different clays are found throughout the country; put to a variety of uses.
- **Dolomite:** Found near Collingwood; is used for agriculture, glassmaking and harbour protection blocks.
- **Greenstone:** Found on the West Coast of the South Island (north Westland and northern Fiordland). Both nephrite and bowenite are called greenstone. It was traditionally prized by the Maori for its hardness, and was used, for example, to make weapons and jewellery. It is still popular for a wide variety of traditional and modern jewellery and ornaments.

All greenstone deposits were returned to Ngai Tahu, the main South Island iwi, as part of their Treaty of Waitangi claim settlement.

- **Limestone:** Found throughout the country; it has a wide range of uses from agriculture to paint filling. Marble (a kind of limestone) is mined in Nelson.
- **Salt:** About 60,000 tonnes of salt per annum is produced at Lake Grassmere, Marlborough.

Income and work

Income summary (2001)

- Market income per person grew slowly from 1986 to 1989, then declined until 1992 before rising again.
- Income inequality has increased over the past decade, mainly due to a larger overall rise in the incomes of high income earners.
- Between 1986 and 1999, real GDP per person grew by 9.5% compared with an OECD average of 29%.
- Average weekly household income was $1021 in 2000/01 (up 6.3% from 1997/98).

Sources of income (Census 2001)

- Wages and salaries were the most common source of income, with nearly six out of 10 people receiving income from this source.
- One in six people received income from self-employment.
- With changes in eligibility, the number of people receiving New Zealand Superannuation or Veterans Pension declined from 441,045 in 1996 to 419,964 in 2001 (nearly one in six people).
- More than nine out of 10 people aged 65 years and over received income from New Zealand Superannuation or Veterans Pension.

Status in employment (Census 2001)

Paid employee	1 296 918
Employer	129 633
Self-employed and without employees	213 117
Unpaid family worker	39 294
Not stated	48 312
Total	**1 727 271**

Levels of income

- The median annual income was $18,500 for the year ended 31 March 2001.
- People in the Wellington region had the highest median annual income at $22,400.
- The Wellington region had the highest portion of people earning an annual income of over $100,000, with one in 25 people.
- The median income for males was $24,900, more than $10,000 above that of $14,500 for females.
- Males in the 40 to 44 age group had the highest median income at $35,900.
- The highest median income for females was in the 45 to 49 age group at $22,000.
- The $10,001–$15,000 income group was the most common, with one in six people (395,106).
- The $30,001–$40,000 income group had one in eight people (311,598).

Savings and financial worth

Key findings from the 2001 Household Savings Survey (Statistics New Zealand):

- New Zealanders aged 18 and older have an estimated total net worth of $367 billion with a median value of $60,000.
- In general, people accumulate net worth as they age. Median net worth was lowest for those aged 18 to 24 years (zero) and highest for the 70 to 74 age group at $177,400.
- Although age is an important factor in the distribution of net worth, there is also significant variation within age bands (e.g. the top 20% of individuals aged 55 to 64 held around 60% of the total net worth of this age group).
- 13% of adults had negative net worth and 22% had net worth over $200,000.

- On average, individuals had $17 of debt for every $100 of assets. The debt ratio was highest for those in the 18 to 24 age group at $63 of debt for every $100 of assets.

Employment and earnings (1999–2001)

(Average March quarter)	1999	2000	2001
Total labour force	1 882 800	1 892 100	1 915 400
Males	1 034 000	1 038 700	1 049 400
Females	848 800	853 400	866 100
Unemployment rate	7.5%	6.7%	5.7%
Males	7.8%	6.6%	5.7%
Females	7.2%	6.7%	5.7%
Average ordinary time weekly earnings ($/wk)			
(at mid-Feb.)	**1999**	**2000**	**2001**
Males	711.94	725.09	751.15
Females	554.04	562.64	572.50
Total both sexes	**638.79**	**649.24**	**666.80**

Unemployment: international comparisons

In mid-2001, New Zealand's unemployment rate was approximated the median of the 22 OECD countries for which data was available at that time.

The Netherlands	2% (lowest of all)
Ireland	4%
UK, Sweden, Japan, NZ	5% (approx.)
Australia	7%

Notable labour force changes over the last two decades

- Education lasting longer.
- More women working in paid jobs for longer period.
- Increased mobility and flexibility.
- Manual work less common – shift to service sector.
- Duration of the working week has decreased.
- Greater variety in the pattern of working hours.
- Paid employment no longer as accessible as it was.
- Unemployment, especially long term, has increased. However, this rate has dropped from a peak of over 10% in the early 1990s to just over 5% by the middle of 2002.

As late as 1966 only 10% of the labour force had some kind of post-school qualification, while 71% had no formal qualifications at all. By 1996, 40% of the labour force had some kind of post-school qualification, while only 26% had no formal qualifications.

Labour force participation

The 2001 Census shows:

- 62% of adults were employed in 2001, compared with 60% in 1996.
- Three out of four of those working were employed full time.
- The number of people employed full time increased by 6% (75,351) from 1996 to 2001.
- The number of people employed part time increased by nearly 6% (21,108) from 1996 to 2001.
- Nearly three out of four part-time workers were female.
- 33% of adults were not in the labour force. This rate was 40% in 1971.
- The labour force participation rate was 67%.

- The most common occupation was sales assistant, with 85,530 people.
- The manufacturing industry had the most workers, with one in seven.
- One in six workers in the agriculture, forestry and fishing industry were from the Waikato region.
- Four in 10 workers in the finance and insurance industry were from the Auckland region.
- One in seven workers in the mining industry were from the Taranaki region and one in eight from the West Coast region.

Employment legislation

Two major recent pieces of employment legislation were the Employment Contracts Act 1991 and the Employment Relations Act 2000.

The 1991 Act said that every employee had to have a contract, but did not have to be represented by a union. The 2000 Act reinstated the right of unions to collectively represent employees. It also had the principle of 'good faith' bargaining at its core. This requires, for example, that both parties:

- Respect each other's roles and the bargaining process.
- Respond to requests for the information needed to carry out these roles.

Hours of work

Unless the parties involved agree otherwise, the working week is fixed at no more than 40 hours, exclusive of overtime.

Holidays

- All workers receive 11 paid public holidays if they fall on working days.
- After one year's employment with the same employer, an employee is entitled to three weeks' paid annual leave.

- Special leave can be taken if an employee, or employee's child, spouse or dependent parent or parent-in-law is sick, or for bereavement.

From 18 March 2002 the minimum wage became:

- Youth rate (16 to 17 year olds) $6.40/hour, $51.20/8-hour day, and $256.00/40-hour week.
- Adult rate (18 years plus) $8.00/hour, $64.00/8-hour day, and $320.00/40-hour week.

Paid parental leave has applied from the first of July 2002, at a maximum rate of $325 gross/week for 12 weeks. A review of this new legislation will take place in 2003.

Qualifications

- There has been a drop in the number of people with no qualifications, from one in three in 1996 to one in four in 2001.
- School Certificate in one or more subjects (or National Certificate level 1) was the highest school qualification for most people, with one in five adults (517,830).
- One in three adults had post-school qualifications.
- One in five adults had a vocational qualification (such as the New Zealand Certificate of Engineering), while one in eight had a degree as their highest post-school qualification.
- Nearly one in five adults in the Wellington region had a degree as their highest qualification.
- The most common field of study for post-school qualifications was nursing, with 58,170 people.
- The information technology field of study for post-school qualifications had 24,009 people.

Spending

Average household spending ($/week)

	1997/98	2000/01
Food, dining out, takeaways	114	125
Rent & home ownership (excl. net capital outlay)	179	181
Running & equipping the home	95	97
Clothing & footwear	27	24
Transport & travel	125	121
Other goods	83	85
Other services	117	125
Total	**739**	**758**

The average weekly household income was $1021 in 2000/01, up 6.3% from 1997/98.

Meals away from home and ready-to-eat foods accounted for 23% of all food expenditure.

Retail trade sales

Retail trade statistics provide information on the state of the New Zealand retail sector, and are a leading indicator of economic activity. Quarterly retail sales reports are available on www.stats.govt.nz.

In June 2002 the retail sales trend continued a pattern of growth evident since June 1998.

Consumers Price Index

The Consumers Price Index (CPI) is possibly New Zealand's best-known statistic and is used to derive measures of inflation. It measures changes in the level of prices of goods and services purchased by private New Zealand households.

It is derived from regularly measuring the prices of a 'basket' of goods and services. The basket's contents are the same quantity and quality each time.

CPI 1999–2001 (percentage change from previous year, June quarter)

	1999	2000	2001	2002
Food	1.9	0.0	6.0	4.1
Housing	–1.5	2.3	–0.6	2.8
All groups	**–0.4**	**2.0**	**3.2**	**2.8**

Infrastructure

Communications

The communications infrastructure in New Zealand has changed and grown greatly in the last 15 years.

New Zealanders have enthusiastically adopted new communication technologies:

- 58% of households in 2000/01 had at least one mobile phone (22% in 1997/98).
- 47% of households in 2000/01 had a home computer (32% in 1997/98).

Telecommunications

- In 1987 the government-owned Post Office split into banking, postal and telecommunications (Telecom New Zealand Ltd) state-owned enterprises.
- In 1989 telecommunication services were opened up to competition.
- In August 1990 Telecom was sold for $4.25 billion. New Zealanders hold about 22% of Telecom shares.
- The 'Kiwi Share Obligation' requires Telecom to provide a local free-calling option for residential customers; residential phone services must remain at least as widespread as at the date of privatisation. Several companies compete with Telecom New Zealand to provide telecommunications services, including TelstraClear, Ihug and Vodaphone.

Access to telecommunication systems

The 2001 Census shows:

- More than nine in every 10 households (96.3%) in private occupied dwellings in New Zealand had access to telecommunication systems.
- Only 3.6% of households had no access to telecommunication systems.

- The percentage of people with access to the Internet has increased steadily. It rose from 42% at the beginning of 1998 to 72% by the end of 2001.
- Access to the Internet was greatest among households with between four and five household members.
- Only 5.7% of households with a total annual gross household income of $15,000 and under had access to the Internet, compared with 71.6% of households with incomes of greater than $40,000.

New Zealand has one of the highest Internet connection rates in the world on a per capita basis.

Internet timeline

1986	International email services through Victoria University of Wellington's dial-up to the University of Calgary, Canada.
1988	International 9600-band circuit between Waikato University and PACCOM in Honolulu.
1989	First New Zealand Internet service provider (ISP).
1990	New Zealand research network linking universities and two government research agencies.
1991	Wellington City Council first local body in the world online. 1200 computers connected to the Internet (July).
1993	First New Zealand websites at Victoria and Waikato Universities.
1994	Tawa Schools Music Festival broadcast live via Internet (August, four weeks before the Rolling Stones do their Internet broadcast). 429 .nz domain name registrations (September). Official government site established November (www.govt.nz)
1996	Over 2000 .nz domain name registrations (November).

1997	More than 10,000 .nz domain name registrations and 4000 websites (April).
1998	Over 500,000 New Zealand users, 16,000 .nz domain name registrations, 8600 websites (February).
1999	182,000 computers connected to the Internet (July). At least 80 ISPs offering New Zealand connection services.
2000	Over 1 million New Zealand users, 46,000 .nz domain name registrations (January).
2001	1.78 million New Zealand users, 46.06% of population (August)* World total estimate 513.41 million.** Asia/Pacific estimate 143.99 million**

* ACNeilsen Netwatch Survey on www.nua.ie/surveys/how_many_online/asia.html
** Nua.com on www.nua.ie/surveys/how_many_online/index.html

Types of organisation on the Internet

The following second level domains are used in New Zealand:

ac.nz	Tertiary educational institutions
co.nz	Companies
cri.nz	Crown Research Institutes
gen.nz	Individuals and organisations which do not fit the other categories
govt.nz	Central government agencies and local and regional councils
iwi.nz	Iwi organisations
mil.nz	Military organisations
net.nz	Internet service providers
org.nz	Non-profit organisations and incorporated societies
school.nz	Schools

Postal services

New Zealand has one of the most liberalised postal markets in the world. On 1 April 1998 the postal market was opened to full competition. To carry out a business involving the carriage of letters, a person or company must be registered as a postal operator with the Ministry of Economic Development. There were 31 registered operators at 25 July 2002.

New Zealand Post Limited

New Zealand Post is a state-owned enterprise. It carries out all regular postal services, and currently maintains the country's electoral rolls. Under a Deed of Understanding with the government, New Zealand Post is required to meet certain social obligations, for example:

- Maintaining a minimum number of delivery points and outlets.
- Not re-introducing the rural delivery fee (abolished on 1 April 1995).

- There were a record 6.7 million letters posted on a 'Free Post Day', 1 July 1996.
- From early February 2002 the first New Zealand Post outlets also became Kiwibank branches. This was a new bank set up by the Labour-Alliance Coalition Government in response to the closing of many bank branches in smaller communities.

Transport

New Zealand is not only remote from other countries, but also has a low-density population scattered over often difficult terrain. International air and telecommunication links have helped overcome the country's isolation, but there is still a heavy reliance on sea transport for overseas trade.

Road transport

- New Zealand has some 95,000 km of road, of which some 10,500 km are state highways and motorways. Nearly 40% of the roads have gravel surfaces.
- Investment in New Zealand's roading and road transport system exceeds that in all other forms of transport.
- Transit New Zealand (www.transit.govt.nz), a Crown entity, is the state highway operator.
- 74 national and provincial road-controlling authorities manage state highways and motorways.
- There are 15,962 km of urban roads and 65,508 km of rural roads and over 16,772 bridges.

Vehicle use

- There are more than 2.7 million road vehicles here. This is the fourth highest ratio of vehicles to population in the world, after the US, Portugal and Luxembourg. Italy and Australia come just below New Zealand. The distance New Zealanders travel on the roads is increasing by an average of 3% each year.
- All vehicles using public roads must be registered.
- Drivers must carry their driver licences with them when they drive on public roads.
- Licences must be renewed at 10-yearly intervals.
- Wearing seat-belts is compulsory in most cases.
- All children under five must be properly restrained by an approved child restraint when travelling in cars and vans.
- All motorcyclists and pillion riders must wear safety helmets.
- Bicycle helmets are compulsory.
- Any driver may be required to give a breath screening test at any time to ensure no alcohol impairment.

- The maximum speed limits for highways and motorways:
  - 100 km/h for cars, motorcycles, vans and light vehicles.
  - 90 km/h for buses, heavy motor and articulated vehicles.
  - 80 km/h for school buses and any vehicles towing trailers.
- A general speed limit of 50 km/h is fixed in all closely populated areas.

KEEP TO THE LEFT when driving.

Vehicle numbers

Motor vehicles licensed	1999	2000	2001
Cars	1 831 118	1 877 850	1 909 480
Motorcycles	42 313	41 234	40 079
Taxis	7 186	7 479	7 181
Total (incl. 'other' vehicles)	**2 668 536**	**2 738 748**	**2 776 448**

According to the 2001 Census, household composition and income influence whether householders can access a motor vehicle.

- Over a quarter of one-person households had no access to a motor vehicle.
- Over half of the households with a total annual gross household income of $15,000 or under had no access to a motor vehicle.
- Less than a tenth of households with a total annual gross household income of over $40,000 had no access to a motor vehicle.
- Of households that had access to three or more motor vehicles, 82% had a total annual gross household income of more than $40,000.

Rail

- In 1993 the state-owned enterprise NZ Rail was sold to the private sector and renamed Tranz Rail (www.tranzrail.co.nz).
- In the 2000/01 financial year:
  - 14.7 million tonnes of freight were carried.
  - 12.6 million urban commuter trips were provided in Wellington and Auckland.
  - 514,000 scenic rail trips were provided.
- Tranz Rail operates a railway network extending over 3912 km.
- There are 2178 bridges and viaducts to carry the railways across the many gorges, rivers and streams.
- The longest railway bridge is that over the Rakaia River, in Canterbury, spanning 1743 m.
- The highest viaduct is the Mohaka, standing 97 m above the Mohaka River on the Napier-Gisborne line.
- There are 149 railway tunnels in New Zealand. The three longest tunnels are:
  - Kaimai (8.9 km) between Tauranga and Morrinsville.
  - Rimutaka (8.8 km) between Upper Hutt and Featherston.
  - Otira (8.5 km), between Otira and Arthur's Pass.

Shipping

- There is a small fleet of coastal ships operated by New Zealand-based operators, with international shipping links provided by foreign operated ships. New Zealand has 13 main ports (operated by port companies). These are: Whangarei; Auckland; Tauranga; Gisborne; New Plymouth; Napier; Wellington; Nelson; Lyttelton; Westport; Timaru; Dunedin; Invercargill. There are also several smaller ports.

- The major export (loading) ports are: Tauranga; New Plymouth; Auckland; Lyttelton; Napier.
- The major import (unloading) ports are: Whangarei; Auckland; Tauranga; Invercargill; Lyttelton.
- Almost 85% of New Zealand exports by value, and over 99% by volume, are carried by sea.
- Around 75% of imports by value and over 99% by volume are sea-borne.

Inter-island ferry services

Tranz Rail operates a ferry service across Cook Strait between Wellington and Picton:

- The *Arahura* and *Aratere* (the Interislander service) carry passengers and vehicles (a three-hour crossing).
- The *Arahanga* carries freight.
- The *Lynx* is a high-speed wave-piercing catamaran (a 135-minute crossing).

Civil aviation

New Zealand is one of the most aviation-oriented nations in the world: in 2000 there were 9040 pilots and 3327 aircraft – one pilot for every 430 people.

- Seven airports offer international services: Auckland; Hamilton; Palmerston North; Wellington; Christchurch; Queenstown; Dunedin. Another 20 airports are serviced by New Zealand's main airlines.
- Since 1986 many airports, formerly partnerships between central and local government, have been restructured as aiport companies, some of which are privately owned.

The first foreign airline operation into New Zealand was Qantas in April 1961 with flights from Cairns, Sydney, Melbourne and Brisbane to Auckland.

International cargo year ended June, tonnes (000)

	2000	2001
Cargo loaded		
NZ sea ports	22 038	22 077
NZ airports	92	91
Total cargo loaded	**22 130**	**22 167**
Cargo unloaded		
NZ sea ports	13 507	14 074
NZ airports	92	88
Total cargo unloaded	**13 600**	**14 162**

Note: Overseas cargo comprises goods freighted to or from New Zealand.

International travel (year ended 30 June)

Arrivals	**2001**	**2002**
Visitors	1 884 480	1 955 700
Returning NZ residents	1 308 490	1 281 500
PLT immigrants	69 490	92 660
All arrivals	3 262 450	3 329 870
Departures		
Visitors	1 873 120	1 941 010
NZ residents (short-term)	1 300 030	1 267 409
PLT emigrants	78 760	59 848
All departures	3 251 900	3 268 270
Net PLT migration	**–9 270**	**32 820**

Note: PLT = permanent and long term.

The net inflow for the June 2002 year offset the combined net outflows for the previous three years by 2400.

New Zealand Customs and Quarantine Services

Check and clear all international travellers and trade entering or leaving New Zealand by air or sea. Biosecurity is particularly important for New Zealand.

Financial institutions and money

- Direct controls on the financial sector have been largely removed since 1984.
- Money market activity has grown rapidly since 1984.
- At the end of June 2001 there were 18 registered banks.
- The Reserve Bank of New Zealand is the central bank, whose functions are:
  - operating monetary policy to maintain price stability.
  - promoting the maintenance of a sound and efficient financial system.
  - meeting the currency needs of the public.

The government has given the Reserve Bank responsibility for keeping inflation low, between 0 and 3% per annum.

Comparison of payment methods (non-cash)

	1999 %	2001 %
MICR (1)	20%	14%
Electronic Credits (2)	20%	19%
Direct Debits	4%	5%
Credit Card (3)	10%	16%
ATM	13%	12%
EFTPOS (4)	33%	34%

Notes: 1. Magnetic Ink Character Recognition (used mostly for verifying cheques). 2. Automatic payments and direct credits. 3. Includes EFTPOS initiated transactions. 4. Debit card transactions on current account.

Money facts

- The present decimal currency system was introduced in 1967, when the dollar replaced pounds, shillings and pence.
- The Reserve Bank has the sole right to issue banknotes and coins.

Housing

The housing sector is a vital part of New Zealand's domestic economy. It is important for health, social stability, and, in New Zealand, 'doing up the house' is a major 'leisure' activity.

Home ownership

	1996	%	2001	%
Owned with mortgage	448 374	36.8	443 274	34.6
Owned without mortgage	394 074	32.4	413 550	32.3

In the 1901 Census there were 170,593 dwellings (only European dwellings were counted). There were also 5116 tents or dwellings with canvas roofs.

Environmental issues: cleaning up

Environmental activities can be seen as part of the country's essential infrastructure.

The New Zealand system of environmental management is intended to be integrated, consistent and effects-based. Three central government agencies have key responsibilities:

- The Ministry for the Environment.
- The Department of Conservation.
- The Parliamentary Commissioner for the Environment.

However, local government carries much of the responsibility for day-to-day environmental management through its role under the Resource Management Act.

Resource Management Act

The Resource Management Act 1991 is the core of the legislation intended to help achieve sustainability. The Act's purpose is to promote the sustainable management of natural and physical resources. It brings together laws governing land, air and water resources by focusing on the environmental effects of human activities.

Current state of the New Zealand environment

Creating our future: sustainable development for New Zealand is a report released by the Commissioner for the Environment in August 2002. The report asserts that the major task in front of New Zealanders (as with the rest of the world) is to redesign our human systems to ensure the continuance of our underpinning ecological ones.

Where New Zealand has done well in the last 10 years has been mostly in community and some local government and business initiatives. 'The big gap in thinking, planning and taking appropriate action until 2000 has been in central government.'

The report gives a number of examples where current systems are not sustainable, such as in New Zealand's use of fossil fuels, and makes recommendations so that change for the better can occur. (This report can be seen on www.pce.govt.nz.)

Other useful sources of environmental information are:

- *The State of New Zealand's Environment 1997* (www.mfe.govt.nz).
- The Ministry of Agriculture and Forestry's Sustainable Resource Use site (www.maf.govt.nz).

Greenhouse gas emissions

- Carbon dioxide (CO_2) emissions from fuel combustion in the energy sector were about 28 million tonnes in 2000.

- The energy sector contributes around 91% of New Zealand's national gross human-made CO_2 emissions, with the remainder from industrial processes. Within the energy sector:
  - 45% is from domestic transport
  - 23% is from industry
  - 18% is from electricity generation.
- New Zealand's overall per capita CO_2 emissions have been estimated to be 8.05 tonnes of CO_2 annually. This compares favourably with those of many other developed countries.
- Other greenhouse gases include nitrous oxide (N_2O) and methane (CH_4) which come from the agricultural sectors.

The Ecological Footprint

The Ecological Footprint is a way of measuring the human impact on nature. It shows how much productive land and water we occupy to produce all the resources we consume and to take in all the waste we make.

Nature provides an average of five acres (2.2 ha) of bioproductive space for every person in the world. Already, humanity's footprint may be over 30% larger than what nature can provide.

Some Footprint comparisons (ha per person)

Angola	0.8	India	1.1
Australia	8.5	New Zealand	9.6
Brazil	2.6	United Kingdom	6.3
China	1.8	United States	12.3
Eritrea	0.3	United Arab Emirates	16.0
France	7.3	**World average**	**2.8**

Primary production

Historical outline

The New Zealand economy can be broadly divided into four phases, with their consequent changes in the nature of primary production.

1. Recovery and transport (19th century). An example is gold, which made up over 50% of exports in the 1860s.
2. Agriculture (20th century), especially meat, wool and dairy products; nearly all went to Britain.
3. Insulationism, triggered by the 1930s Depression. The government set up import licensing and exchange controls.
4. Diversification (latter 20th century). Export markets and export products diversified, and the economy opened up to foreign competition.

Agriculture, horticulture and forestry

Farming, horticulture and forestry together provide the greatest part of New Zealand's export earnings.

Land area and use, ha (000)

Grazing, arable, fodder and fallow land	13 863
Land in horticulture	129
Plantations of exotic timber	1 799
Total area of New Zealand	**26 870**

Total pasture and arable land makes up 51% of the total land area of New Zealand. Others are:

Natural forest	24%
Planted forests	6%
Other land	19%

GDP contribution (March year, $ m)*

	1996	2001
Agriculture	4 947	6 018
Forestry and logging	1 201	1 382
Food and beverage manufacturing	4 869	5 268
Wood and paper products manufacturing	1 953	2 317
Total	**92 680**	**104 317**

*Constant 1995/96 prices.

The volume of plantation timber available for export is expected to increase 74% between 1996 and 2010.

Primary products by value

Agricultural, horticultural and forestry exports were valued at $20.6 billion and accounted for 66% of New Zealand's total exports for the year ended March 2002:

	$ m
Dairy	6 242
Meat and meat products	4 491
Forestry products	3 650
Other pastoral products	2 868
Horticultural products	1 995
Wool	943
Other agricultural products	456

New Zealand primary producers are almost totally exposed to market forces. They receive no government subsidies and often have to compete with subsidised production from other countries.

Employment in primary production

Number of people employed in:

Agriculture (as at 1998)	
Sheep farming	18 850
Beef cattle	10 280
Dairy cattle	42 500
Other livestock and grain farming	26 370
Other crop growing	920
Services to agriculture	16 120
Total	**115 040**

Horticulture (as at 1998)	
Fruit growing	18 240
Vegetable growing	7 970
Flower and flower seed growing	3 060
Plant nurseries	3 390
Total	**32 660**

Forestry (as at February 2001)	
Forestry activities	1 620
Logging activities	4 710
Services to forestry	3 700
Sawmills	7 420
Chipmills	35
Plywood and veneer manufacturing	1 970
Other	4 860
Total forestry and first stage processing	**24 315**

Agriculture

Pastoral agriculture is practised throughout New Zealand. Stock graze outside all year round. Such farming practices, geographical isolation, robustly enforced legislation on animal health and welfare, and strict biosecurity measures all reduce the chances of serious animal health problems.

New Zealand has never had an outbreak of foot and mouth disease; it has also been classified in the lowest risk category for BSE.

Agricultural products by value

Agricultural exports totalled $15 billion for the year ended March 2002. The major contributors were:

- Dairy products $6242 million.
- Meat and meat products $4491 million.
- Pastoral based exports $2,868 million (casein, hides/skins, carpets, etc).
- Wool $943 million.
- Other agricultural products $456 million (cereals, meat meals, pet food, etc).

Total livestock numbers (000)

	1975	1995	1999
Sheep	55 320	48 816	45 680
Dairy cattle	2 998	4 090	4 316
Beef cattle	6 294	5 183	4 644
Deer	–	1179	1 677
Pigs	422	431	369
Goats	–	1 063	186

The best sheep farms can carry up to 25 sheep per hectare throughout the year. The best dairy farms carry 3.5 cows per hectare throughout the year.

Total farms by type (as at 30 June 1999)

Grain growing	543
Grain-sheep and grain-beef cattle farming	2 085
Sheep-beef cattle farming	10 911
Sheep farming	9 417
Beef cattle farming	12 141
Dairy cattle farming	15 951
Poultry farming (meat)	123
Poultry farming (eggs)	84
Pig farming	267
Horse farming	621
Deer farming	1 917
Mixed livestock	4 323
Horticulture and fruit growing	1 917
Other	6 906
Unknown	13 176
Total	**80 376**

Dairy industry

Average herd size	236
Average farm size	93 ha
Production per hectare	750 kg milk solids
Total number of dairy farms	15 951
Total number of cows	4.3 million

Waikato, Taranaki and Northland regions are the top three dairy producers.

Dairy exports year ended March 2002 ($ m)

Wholemilk powder	2 248.0
Cheese	1 459.1
Skim and buttermilk powder	1 297.4
Butter	1 090.6
Dairy products	147.2

The Fonterra Co-operative Group Ltd

Fonterra was formed in 2001 from the merger of the New Zealand Dairy Group and Kiwi Co-operative Dairies. The company:

- Is New Zealand's largest company.
- Controls nearly all New Zealand dairy exports.
- Comprises approximately 100 smaller companies.
- Employs approximately 20,000 people.
- Operates in 120 countries (every continent except Antarctica).

Meat

- Meat industry products are New Zealand's second largest export income earner.
- They comprise about 17% of merchandise exports.
- Main meat exports are lamb, mutton and beef.
- About 91% of lamb, 79% of mutton and 83% of beef produced in New Zealand in 1998–99 was exported overseas.
- Major meat markets are:
  - Lamb: UK, Germany, France, Saudi Arabia and US.
  - Mutton: UK, Germany, South Korea and France.
  - Beef: US, Canada, Japan, South Korea and Taiwan.

- Most venison is exported to 51 markets. The top three markets are Germany, the US and Belgium.
- The domestic market absorbs over 99% of pigmeat and poultry produced in New Zealand. Canterbury is New Zealand's top lamb producer, followed by the Southland, Wanganui and Otago regions.

- The first shipment of frozen meat was on the refrigerated clipper *Dunedin*. It left on 15 February 1882, from Port Chalmers, Dunedin bound for England.
- New Zealand accounts for about 53% of the world export trade in sheepmeat. It accounts for about 10% of all world beef exports.
- Consumption of chicken has increased, from 14 kg per person 10 years ago, to almost 31 kg in 2001.

Wool

- New Zealand is the world's largest producer of crossbred (strong) wool.
- It is estimated that 34% of New Zealand wool is used in machine-made carpets, 12% in hand-knotted and hand-tufted carpets, 44% in apparel, and 10% in other uses.
- The largest importers of New Zealand wool were China, the UK, India, Germany and Belgium (1997–98).

New Zealand wool types reflect the different sheep breeds. Some sheep have coarse, strong wool, meaning that each wool fibre is thick. Others have fine wool (thin fibres) or wool of medium thickness.

The diameter of wool fibre is measured in microns (a micron is one millionth of a metre and is a standard textile fibre measurement):

- Crossbred wool is mostly greater than 31 microns in fibre diameter.

- Halfbred and Corriedale wool falls in the range of 25–31 microns.
- Merino wool is 24 microns and less.

Fine, light, warm clothing is now being produced by combining fur from the possum (a national ecological pest) with merino wool.

Crops and horticulture

In recent years there have been significant increases in the areas planted in horticulture and other crops.

- New Zealand's horticultural exports were valued at $2 billion for the March 2002 year (up 2% on the previous year).
- Land under horticultural production totalled 128,700 ha as at 30 June 2000.

Main horticultural crops

Kiwifruit

- Exports of fresh kiwifruit totalled $578 million for the year ended March 2002.
- New Zealand's kiwifruit industry is developing new flavours, flesh colours and textures. The tropical tasting gold kiwifruit variety marketed as Zespri™ GOLD was launched in 1998.
- The area planted in kiwifruit, as at June 2000, was estimated at 12,184 ha.
- The Bay of Plenty is the top growing region. In June 2000, there were 1782 kiwifruit growers in the Bay of Plenty. Plantings of kiwifruit covered 8892 ha.
- The major export markets for kiwifruit are the European Union and Japan.

New Zealand supplies around one quarter of the world's kiwifruit under the Zespri™ brand. (See www.zespri.com.)

Apple and pears

- Apple and pear growers were New Zealand's second largest horticultural export earners for the March 2002 year.
- Exports of fresh apples were valued at $360 million for the year ended March 2002.
- There were 14,114 ha planted in apples as at 30 June 2000.
- New Zealand's major export markets for apples are the European Union, especially the UK, and the US.
- The main varieties grown are Braeburn, Gala, Royal Gala and Fuji. Production of the New Zealand-developed Pacific Rose is increasing.
- The main growing regions are Hawke's Bay and Tasman.

Almost 70% of the New Zealand pipfruit industry's export income is derived from the apple varieties Braeburn, Gala and Royal Gala, which were all developed in this country.

Wine

- The New Zealand wine industry has grown at a dramatic rate in the last two decades. Wineries can now be found in 10 out of 12 New Zealand regions.
- The area in wine grapes has doubled since 1990 to 12,665 ha.
- In 1990 wine exports were valued at $20 million. For the year ended March 2002, wine exports totalled $244 million.
- The key export markets for New Zealand wine are the UK, Australia and the US.
- Premium prices are achieved by New Zealand wines on world markets.
- Chardonnay and sauvignon are the major white grape varieties grown in New Zealand. The major premium red grape varieties are pinot noir and cabernet sauvignon.

- Marlborough, Gisborne and Hawke's Bay are the major grape producing areas, but the Wairarapa and Central Otago are becoming well-known, especially for their award-winning pinot noir wines.

Fruit and vegetables

- Fresh vegetable exports, for the year ended March 2002, totalled $245 million, frozen vegetables $152 million and dried vegetables $45 million.
- Exports of fresh fruit were valued at $1052 million for the March 2002 year.
- Land in outdoor fruit was estimated at 52,927 ha, an increase of 13% when compared to 1994 when the last horticultural census was held.
- Land in outdoor vegetables, over the same period, increased by 3% to 56,809 ha.

Cut flowers

- The value of cut flower exports averaged 10% growth per year since 1990, although in the last few years export values have not been as high as in the mid-1990s.
- Valued at $48 million for the year ended March 2002, cut flowers accounted for 63% of New Zealand's total exports of trees and live plants.

> Manuka honey is very effective as an antiseptic dressing. It is one of a number of New Zealand native honeys with wide national and international consumer appeal.

Forestry

- Forests cover about 30% or 8.1 million ha of New Zealand's land area.
- About 6.4 million ha is in indigenous forest. Nearly all indigenous forest is protected from harvesting.

- 1.799 million ha is in planted production forests, of which:
  - 89% is radiata pine, of which about one third is in the central North Island.
  - 5% is Douglas fir.
  - about 3% are hardwoods, notably eucalypts.
- 588,000 ha of forest have been established since 1990.
- An estimated 33,600 ha of new forest was established in 2000.
- Almost all areas of forest harvested are replanted.
- The potential sustainable wood supply available from New Zealand's planted production forests could increase from about 18 million cu m currently to more than 30 million cu m by 2006.

Export earnings for forestry products

New Zealand's forestry exports were valued at $3697 million for the December 2001 year (up 3% on the previous year).

Exports of forestry products 1996 and 2001 ($ m)

	1996	2001
Sawn timber	370	802
Fibreboard	171	290
Furniture	33	57
Mouldings etc	51	86

Main destinations for forestry products 2001 ($ m)

Australia	917
Japan	767
Korea	548
US	491
China	362

In the year ended 31 December 2001 New Zealand exported 7.2 million cu m of logs. The production of sawn timber has gone up by 69% since 1991.

Main destinations for sawn timber 2001

	Million cu m	Value ($ m)
Korea	4.1	431
Japan	1.5	191
China	0.9	98
Philippines	0.2	25
India	0.2	19

Fishing

- Seafood exports are currently New Zealand's fourth largest export earner. In 2000, 280 million kg of seafood products left the country, worth a total of $1.43 billion to the economy. This was a 7% increase on the 1999 earnings.
- New Zealand's Exclusive Economic Zone (EEZ) is one of the largest in the world at 1.3 million square nautical miles, an area 15 times the country's landmass.
- The waters are relatively deep, with less than one-third shallower than 1000 m, the depth where most fishing takes place.
- The waters are not very productive but support over 1000 species of marine fish, about 100 of which are commercially significant.
- The main method used to manage fisheries is known as the Quota Management System, which sets catch limits for each fish stock.
- Rights to harvest fish for sale are acquired by purchasing or leasing quota.

- The Ministry of Fisheries (MFish) is responsible for the sustainable utilisation of fisheries (see www.fish.govt.nz).
- Maori control approximately a third by volume of the fishing quota, through their $175 million half share of Sealord Products Ltd.

In late 1992 the Crown agreed to fund Maori in a 50/50 joint venture with Brierley Investments Ltd to bid for Sealord Products Ltd, New Zealand's biggest fishing company. The Deed also promised Maori 20% of quota for new species added to the Quota Management System. In return, Maori agreed that all their current and future claims in respect of commercial fishing rights were fully satisfied and discharged.

Major export fish species 2000 ($ m)

Hoki	311
Green-lipped mussels	169
Rock lobster	129
Orange roughy	84
Ling	78
Abalone/paua	66
Squid	42
Snapper	37
Hake	34
Salmon	29

Major markets for fish

Traditionally Japan has been New Zealand's biggest export market, taking up to a third of our exports in 1992. The United States and the European Union have also become key markets, and with Japan take well over half our seafood exports.

Largest export markets for fish in 2000 ($ m)

Japan	318
US	258
European Union	219
Hong Kong	169
Australia	167
China	78
Korea	46
Singapore	43
Taiwan	30
Thailand	18

Aquaculture

- Green-lipped mussels, salmon and Pacific oysters continue to be the mainstay of New Zealand's aquaculture industry.
- Aquaculture is the fastest-growing seafood industry, already making up about 15% of seafood exports.

In November 2001 a two-year moratorium was imposed on new aquafarming ventures. This is so that legislation, research and local body planning can respond to the rapid growth in the industry.

Tourism

New Zealand is famed for its natural beauty and space, the intriguing animal and plant life, and for its outdoors lifestyle and culture.

There is a great diversity of scenery and experiences within the country. Traditionally, the most popular visitor sites have been Milford Sound, Queenstown, the West Coast glaciers and the geysers and hot springs of the central North Island. However, more international and domestic tourists are now exploring further. For example, many once-isolated farms now have additional income through visitor hosting.

Popular activities

- Adventure tourism: bungy-jumping, white-water rafting, jet-boating etc.
- Biking: mountain biking, touring.
- Hiking, especially through the national parks.
- Whale-watching.
- Recreational fishing (see www.fishnhunt.co.nz).
- Skiing.
- Farm visits and homestays.
- Marae visits.
- Winery tours.
- Museums and historic sites.
- Shopping: antiques, designer clothing, New Zealand crafts.

Events

Sporting and cultural events also put New Zealand in the international spotlight. There are many wine, food, arts and flower festivals, Maori cultural competitions, triathlons and rugby matches. Conferences and conventions also generate considerable business for many cities and towns.

Overseas visitor arrivals by country (top 10, 2002)

Australia	624 644
United Kingdom	228 086
United States	194 798
Japan	150 343
Korea	97 880
China	65 110
Germany	48 557
Canada	38 528
Taiwan	36 865
Singapore	32 682

Value of tourism (year ended March)

	1999	2000
Tourism expenditure ($ m)	11 939	13 176
Direct tourism value added ($ m)	4 343	4 809
Indirect tourism value added ($ m)	4 312	4 739
Total tourism value added ($ m)	8 655	9 548
Full-time equivalent persons directly engaged in tourism	83 317	94 024
Tourism's direct contribution to GDP	4.6%	4.9%

Note: figures rounded.

Tourism highlights

- Tourism expenditure grew by 14.8% between 1997 and 2000.
- The number of persons directly engaged as a result of tourism increased by 9.6% between 1997 and 2000.

- Direct tourism value added (also known as tourism's direct contribution to GDP) grew by 14.6% between 1997 and 2000. Total industry contribution to GDP increased by 9.7% during the same period.
- Direct tourism value added made up 4.9% of total industry contribution to GDP in 2000.
- GST paid on goods and services directly consumed by tourists grew from $851 million in 1997 to $972 million in 2000.

In the last third of 2001 short-term visitor numbers to New Zealand dropped due to the events of 11 September in New York, and the collapse of the Ansett Australia airline. However, by December the numbers of visitors had risen rapidly. In the year ended December 2001, there were still 1.910 million visitor arrivals, up 121,000 or 7% on the previous year.

Overseas tourist accommodation

Of the accommodation nights spent by international visitors, the estimated percentages of nights spent in each of the following (1999) were:

- 37% private homes
- 16% hotels
- 12% backpacker hostels
- 10% motels
- 7% student accommodation
- 6% campervans or camping grounds
- 7% rented homes or time shares
- 2% farm or homestays
- The balance in other forms of accommodation such as luxury lodges, national parks or in transit.

Manufacturing

There has been major reform of the business environment for manufacturing. All import licensing was removed in 1992. In 1997 the National Government planned to reduce all tariffs to zero before 2010, but in 2000 the Labour Government froze all tariffs until at least 2005.

Major manufacturing industry groups

- Food
- Wine
- Textiles and apparel
- Carpet
- Footwear

Employment % by industry type (1999)

Food, beverage, tobacco	25.0%
Machinery & equipment	18.3%
Metal products	11.5%
Wood & paper products	10.3%
Printing, publishing & recorded media	8.9%
Textile, clothing, footwear, leather	8.8%
Petroleum, coal & chemical products	8.3%
Other manufacturing	5.9%
Non-metallic mineral products	2.9%

The motor vehicle assembly industry began to decline in 1987, when tariffs were cut on imported used cars. The last plant, Honda in Nelson, closed in October 1998.

Manufacturing sector performance

	1997	1998	1999
GDP at 1991–92 prices ($ m)	87 211	88 949	88 923
Growth of GDP contribution	0.6%	2.4%	–3.7%

- In contrast to the decline in manufacturing in 1999 shown in the above table, the industry showed an increase in sales of processed goods and services of 9.5% in 2000.
- The Quarterly Economic Survey of Manufacturing also reported an increase in sales of processed goods and services for the year to March 2000.
- Other purchases and operating income, which includes purchases of raw materials, showed an increase of 10.3%.
- Purchases of fixed assets rose by 17.3% compared with a 10.7% fall in the previous year.
- This major turnaround in the acquisition of fixed assets indicates strong business confidence in the manufacturing industries.
- Salaries and wages paid to employees picked up 4.3% from a fall of 0.7% in 1999, while business demographic statistics for manufacturing indicate employment increased by 5.9% between February 1999 and 2000.
- The manufacturing industry is the largest employer with 234,890 full-time equivalent persons engaged as at February 2001.

Science and technology

Government-funded science agencies

Some Crown Research Institutes

- AgResearch (www.agresearch.cri.nz).
- Agricultural and Marketing Research and Development Trust (www.agmardt.org.nz).
- Crop and Food Research Limited (www.crop.cri.nz).
- Forest Research (www.forestresearch.co.nz).
- HortResearch (www.hort.cri.nz).
- Industrial Research Limited (www.irl.cri.nz).
- Institute of Environmental Science and Research Limited (www.esr.cri.nz).
- Institute of Geological and Nuclear Sciences Limited (www.gns.cri.nz).
- Landcare Research New Zealand Limited (www.landcare.cri.nz).
- National Institute of Water and Atmospheric Research Limited (www.niwa.cri.nz).

The Royal Society of New Zealand (www.rsnz.govt.nz) aims to foster a culture supportive of science and technology and to give expert advice on important public issues.

Other research organisations

- Carter Observatory (astronomy) (www.vuw.ac.nz/~carter).
- The Cawthron Institute: research into marine and fresh-water microbiology and ecology (www.cawthron.org.nz).
- The Malaghan Institute of Medical Research.

Government departments

Government departments carry out research and development to support their own activities. This includes research that supports the development and effective implementation of policy.

Tertiary institutions

The eight universities carry out basic and strategic research and make substantial contributions in applied science and technology fields. Several universities also have formal links with CRIs.

Some 24 polytechnics offer certificate and diploma courses in a variety of subjects related to science and technology, including agriculture, horticulture, forestry, viticulture, engineering, manufacturing and software engineering.

A resourceful people: Kiwi ingenuity

New Zealanders pride themselves on their flexible and inventive approach to challenges. The 'number 8 (fencing) wire', used in many unconventional ways, is a symbol of that inventiveness, and of the isolated pioneers who had to 'make do' with any materials at hand.

A few Kiwi inventions

Several aeroplanes from 1899 (Richard Pearse).
Aeroplane with tilting engine (anticipating the Harrier jump jet), Pearse, 1940s.
Stamp-vending machine (Robert Dickie).
Hamilton jetboat (Sir William Hamilton).
Spiral hairpin (Ernest Godward).
Britten motorcycle (John Britten).
Disposable syringe (Colin Murdoch).
Tranquilliser gun (Colin Murdoch).
Bungy-jumping (A.J. Hackett & Henry Van Asch).
Two-drawer dishwasher (Fisher & Paykel Ltd).
Spreadable butter (NZ Dairy Research Institute).

The most famous New Zealand scientist is Ernest Rutherford, who won the Nobel Prize in 1908 for his work on the nuclear theory of the atom.

Information technology

- Total value of sales of Information Technology (IT) goods and services in the 2000 financial year was estimated at $11.1 billion, an increase of 6.9% from the previous year.
- Sales of IT goods and services have had a mean growth rate of 10.4% every year since 1994.
- Exports of IT goods and services have increased 10.7% to $0.9 billion between the 1999 and 2000 financial years.
- Exports of software increased by 13.9% or $13.8 million, to reach $112.8 million in the 2000 financial year. Software exports have increased by $51.8 million since 1996.

Overseas merchandise trade

Exports by country (FOB, $ m, year ended June)

	2000	2001
Australia	5 503	6 083
US	3 739	4 644
Japan	3 371	4 277
UK	1 609	1 552
Republic of Korea	1 172	1 405
People's Republic of China	731	1 114
Hong Kong (SAR)	710	847
All merchandise exports	**26 027**	**31 939**

Imports by country ($ m, year ended June)

	2000	2001
Australia	6 843	7 010
US	5 127	5 298
Japan	3 474	3 427
People's Republic of China	1 630	2 149
Germany	1 182	1 419
UK	1 161	1 187
Malaysia	717	966
All merchandise imports	**29 193**	**31 927**

Note: Includes insurance and freight.
Source: Statistics New Zealand.

Exports by commodity (FOB, $ m, year ended June)

	2000	2001
Milk powder, butter & cheese	3 975	5 811
Meat & edible offal	3 376	4 179
Wood & wood articles	2 018	2 219
Fish, crustaceans & molluscs	1 223	1 366
Mechanical machinery	1 125	1 327
Aluminium and articles thereof	1 116	1 295
Casein & caseinates	803	1 213
All merchandise exports	**26 027**	**31 939**

Imports by commodity ($ m, year ended June)

	2000	2001
Mechanical machinery	3 807	4 111
Vehicles, parts and accessories	3 594	3 667
Mineral fuels	2 319	3 545
Electrical machinery	2 938	3 380
Textiles and textile articles	1 580	1 738
Plastic and plastic articles	1 191	1 337
Optical, medical and measuring equipment	845	984
All merchandise imports	**29 193**	**31 927**

Note: Includes insurance and freight.
Source: Statistics New Zealand.

National finance

Balance of payments ($ m, year ended 31 March)

	2000	2001
Balance on goods	–812	2 119
Balance on services	–485	–263
Balance on income	–6 604	–7 736
Balance on current transfers	509	466
Balance of current account	–7 391	–5 414
Net transactions in reserves	–172	5
Official overseas reserves end of March	7 877	8 566
NZ investment abroad	5 811	12 156
Foreign investment in NZ	9 981	17 440
Net international investment position	–87 084	–84 344
Net international debt	–80 378	–65 376

National accounts aggregates ($ m, year ended 31 March)

	2000	2001
Gross Domestic Product	105 641	112 316
Gross National Expenditure	107 002	110 076
Gross Fixed Capital Formation	21 019	21 477
Gross Domestic Product chain-volume series expressed in 1995/96 prices	102 267	104 932

Note: Upgraded New Zealand System of National Accounts.
Source: Statistics New Zealand.

Central government finance ($ m, year ended June)

	2000	2001
Revenue		
Direct taxation	21 499	23 863
Indirect taxation	12 536	12 875
Compulsory fees, fines, penalties and levies	376	385
Total revenue levied through the Crown's Sovereign Power	34 411	37 123
Total revenue earned through the Crown's operations	2 115	2 369
Total revenue	**36 526**	**39 492**
Total expenses	**36 171**	**38 186**
Revenue less expenses	**355**	**1 306**
Net surplus/deficit, less distributions, attributable to State-owned enterprises and Crown entities	1 094	103
Operating balance	**1 449**	**1 409**
Public debt outstanding		
Due in foreign currency	7 728	7 646
Due in NZ currency	28 313	29 115
Total public debt	**36 041**	**36 761**

Source: Statistics New Zealand.

Information for visitors

(See www.purenz.com and pages 217–18 for driving laws.)

Money

New Zealand's unit of currency is the New Zealand dollar (NZ$). Coins have values of 5, 10, 20 and 50 cents, $1 and $2; notes have values of $5, $10, $20, $50 and $100.

There is no restriction on the amount of foreign currency that can be brought in or taken out of New Zealand. However, every person who carries more than NZ$10,000 in cash in or out of New Zealand is required to complete a Border Cash Report.

Foreign currency can easily be exchanged at banks, some hotels and Bureau de Change kiosks, which are found at international airports and most city centres.

All major credit cards can be used in New Zealand. Travellers' cheques are accepted at hotels, banks and some stores.

Business hours

Business: Monday to Friday 8.00 am – 5.00 pm
Trading Banks: Monday to Friday 9.00 am – 4.30 pm
Shopping: Monday to Friday 9.00 am – 5.00 pm
Late nights Thursday or Friday to 9.00 pm
Saturday 10.00 am – 4.00 pm (most shops)
Sunday 11.00 am – 3.00 pm (most shops)
Post Office: Monday to Friday 9.00 am – 5.00 pm
Saturday 9.00 am – 12 noon (some only)
Convenience stores: or 'dairies' are generally open 7.00 am – 10.00 pm seven days a week.
Service stations: or petrol stations are often open 24 hours.

Taxes and tipping

GST (Goods and Services Tax) of 12.5% is applied to the cost of all goods and services and is generally included in all prices.

GST cannot be claimed back from purchases; however, it is not included in duty free prices or where the goods are posted by a retailer to an international visitor's home address. GST is not included in international airfares purchased in New Zealand.

Gratuities (tips) are not expected, but if a visitor wishes to leave a tip for outstanding service, it is certainly appreciated. Service charges are not added to hotel or restaurant accounts.

Emergency services

In emergencies, dial 111 to summon police, fire or ambulance services. DO NOT DIAL 911.

Electricity and water

New Zealand's AC electricity supply operates at 230/240 volts (50 hertz), the same as Australia. Most hotels and motels also provide 110 volt, 20 watt, AC sockets for electric razors. An adaptor is necessary to operate all other electrical equipment.

Tap (faucet) water in New Zealand is fresh, treated and is very safe to drink. City water is both chlorinated and fluoridated. To prevent any problems, when travelling in the back-country (tramping, camping or the like), ensure water is boiled or otherwise treated before drinking.

New Zealand has very strict biosecurity measures to protect our unique land and its resources. (See www.quarantine.govt.nz).

Sources and further information

The following articles, books and websites are only a small selection of material available on New Zealand. For example, there are many excellent, highly informative and accessible books on New Zealand natural history, few of which could be listed here. The books and websites listed are those that were direct sources for the information in this book, or which are a good source of general information for readers.

Environment

Bishop, N., 1992. *Natural History of New Zealand.* Hodder & Stoughton, Auckland.

Chin, T.J., 2001. 'Distribution of the glacial water resources of New Zealand' in *Journal of Hydrology (NZ) 40(2)I*, New Zealand Hydrological Society (2001) pp. 139–187.

Hutching, G., 1998. *The Natural World of New Zealand.* Viking, Auckland.

Kirkpatrick, R., 1999. *Bateman Contemporary Atlas New Zealand.* David Bateman, Auckland.

McKinnon, M. (ed), 1997, 1999. *Bateman New Zealand Historical Atlas.* David Bateman, Auckland, in association with the Department of Internal Affairs.

Statistics New Zealand, 2000. *New Zealand Official Yearbook 2000.* David Bateman, Auckland.

Vegetation

Bishop, N., 1992. *Natural History of New Zealand.* Hodder & Stoughton, Auckland.

Brockie, R., 1992. *A Living New Zealand Forest.* David Bateman, Auckland.

Druett, J., *Exotic Intruders – the Introduction of Plants and*

Animals into New Zealand from Statistics New Zealand, 1990. *New Zealand Official Yearbook 1990.*

Salmon, J.T., 1980. *The Native Trees of New Zealand.* Reed, Auckland.

Wildlife

Baker, A., 1990. *Whales and Dolphins of New Zealand and Australia.* Victoria University Press, Wellington.

Bateman New Zealand Encyclopaedia 5th Edition. (2000) David Bateman, Auckland.

Bishop, N., 1992. *Natural History of New Zealand.* Hodder & Stoughton, Auckland.

Daniel, M. and Baker, A., 1986. *Collins Guide to the Mammals of New Zealand.* Collins, .

Gill, B., 1991. *New Zealand's Extinct Birds.* Random Century, Auckland.

Hutching, G., 1998. *The Natural World of New Zealand.* Viking, Auckland.

King, C.M. (ed), 1990. *The Handbook of New Zealand Mammals.* Oxford University Press, Auckland.

Lindsey, T. and Morris, R., 2000. *Collins Field Guide to New Zealand Wildlife.* HarperCollins, Auckland.

Molloy J. et al., 2001. *Classifying species according to threat of extinction: A system for New Zealand.* Department of Conservation, Wellington.

Moon, G., 1994. *The Reed Field Guide to New Zealand Wildlife.* Reed, Auckland.

Morrisey, M. (ed), 1993. *NZ's Top Ten.* Moa Beckett, Auckland. (On the only snakes in New Zealand.)

Patterson, G. in 'Skinks on the Edge', *New Zealand Geographic Number 47, July–September 2000*, pp. 62–81.

Peat, N. and Patrick, B., 1999. *Wild Central.* University of Otago Press, Dunedin.

Taylor, M., 1993. *Old Blue, the Rarest Bird in the World.* Ashton Scholastic, Auckland.

Walker, A., 2000. *The Reed Handbook of Common Insects.* Reed, Auckland.

History

Ballara, A., 1996. 'Te Kingitanga: The People of the Maori King Movement', *The Dictionary of New Zealand Biography.* Also on www.dnzb.govt.nz

Binney, J., 1990. 'Te Kooti Arikirangi Te Turuki ?–1893'. *Dictionary of New Zealand Biography.* Volume One (1769–1869).

Keenan, D., 1993. 'Te Whiti-o-Rongomai III, Erueti ?–1907'. *Dictionary of New Zealand Biography.* Volume Two (1870–1900).

McKinnon, M. (ed), 1997, 1999. *Bateman New Zealand Historical Atlas.* David Bateman, Auckland, in association with the Department of Internal Affairs.

Statistics New Zealand, 2000. *New Zealand Official Yearbook 2000.* David Bateman, Auckland.

Social Welfare

Crampton, P. et al., 2000. *Degrees of Deprivation in New Zealand. An atlas of socio-economic difference.* David Bateman, Auckland.

Statistics New Zealand (compiled by Pullar, V.), 1995. *Facts New Zealand.* Statistics New Zealand, Wellington.

Health

Sexual and Reproductive Health Strategy Phase One, 2001. Ministry of Health, Wellington.

Language

Brougham, A.E. & Reed, A.W. (revised by Karetu, T.), 1996. *The Reed Pocket Maori Proverbs.* Reed, Auckland.

Orsman, H., 1994. *The Beaut Little Book of New Zealand Slang.* Reed, Auckland.

Orsman, H. (ed), 1998. *Dictionary of New Zealand English.* Oxford University Press, Auckland.

Resources and economy

Hortresearch, 2001. *New Zealand Horticultural Facts and Figures 2001.* Hortresearch, Palmerston North

Statistics New Zealand, 2000. *New Zealand Official Yearbook 2000.* David Bateman, Auckland.

Websites and other sources

Section 1: Natural history

Southern stars

Dr Nicholas Jones, personal communication

Royal Astronomical Society of New Zealand: www.rasnz.org.nz

Geological history

Caves

New Zealand Speleological Society records.

Geographical extremes

www.linz.govt.nz

www.tourisminfo.govt.nz

Volcanoes

www.gns.cri.nz

Climate

www.niwa.cri.nz

www.metservice.co.nz

El Niño

http://katipo.niwa.cri.nz/ClimateFuture/El_Nino.htm

www.pmel.noaa.gov/toga-tao/el-nino-story.html

www.climatechange.govt.nz/sp

Ozone and ultraviolet light
www.niwa.cri.nz

Plants and animals
www.doc.govt.nz
Origins of New Zealand plants and animals
www.mfe.govt.nz
www.doc.govt.nz
Worst New Zealand pests
www.landcare.cri.nz
Plants and wildlife
www.landcare.cri.nz
www.kauri-museum.com
www.forest-
bird.org.nz/biosecurity/cats/policy_background.asp
Bird extinctions
www.nzbirds.com
Rare and endangered birds
www.nzbirds.com
www.doc.govt.nz
www.kiwirecovery.org.nz
www.panda.org/resources/publications/species/underthreat/chathamrobin.htm
www.kakapo.net
www.kakaporecovery.org.nz
www.yellow-eyedpenguin.org.nz
http://users.capu.net/~kwelch/pp/species/yellow-eyed.html
Flightless birds
www.forest-bird.org.nz
www.nzbirds.com
Native mammals
www.doc.govt.nz
http://nzwhaledolphintrust.tripod.com/home

Reptiles and amphibians
www.doc.govt.nz
www.bigjude.com/Tuatara.html
http://mtbruce.doc.govt.nz/tuatara.htm
Invertebrates
www.doc.govt.nz

National parks and reserves
www.doc.govt.nz
www.unesco.org/whc/heritage.htm

Section 2: People

History
www.tourisminfo.govt.nz
www.nzhistory.net.nz
www.zealand.org.nz/history.htm
Dictionary of New Zealand Biography: www.dnzb.govt.nz
Electronic Journal of Australian and New Zealand History: www.jcu.edu.au/aff/history
National Archives of New Zealand: www.archives.govt.nz
New Zealand National Register of Archives and Manuscripts: www.nram.org.nz
Timeframes: timeframes.natlib.govt.nz
Peoples of New Zealand
www.stats.govt.nz
www.zealand.org.nz/history.htm
Iwi (Maori tribes)
Census 2001 at www.stats.govt.nz
Metge, J., 1967. *The Maoris of New Zealand*. Routledge and K. Paul, London.
Moriori
www.zealand.org.nz/history.htm
www.aotearoalive.com

Treaty of Waitangi
www.ots.govt.nz
www.knowledge-basket.co.nz/waitangi/welcome.html
www.zealand.org.nz/history.htm

Government
Ministry of Social Policy: www.mosp.govt.nz.
The Legislature (Parliament)
www.govt.co.nz
www.ps.parliament.govt.nz
www.decisionmaker.co.nz/guide/parliament
'Report of the Representation Commission 2002', on: www.elections.org.nz
Executive
www.govt.nz
www.dpmc.govt.nz
www.decisionmaker.co.nz/guide/Government
www.treasury.govt.nz
The judiciary
www.courts.govt.nz
www.decisionmaker.co.nz/guide/parliament
Corruption Perceptions Index
Transparency International: www.transparency.org
Citizens' Initiated Referenda
www.elections.org.nz
Local government
www.elections.org.nz
www.lgnz.co.nz/localgovt
www.localgovt.co.nz
New Zealand honours system
www.dpmc.govt.nz/honours/intro/index.html
National emblems and anthems
www.govt.nz/aboutnz/icons.php3

International relations

www.cia.gov/cia/publications/factbook
www.mfat.govt.nz
www.nzaid.govt.nz
www.oecd.org

Defence

www.cia.gov/cia/publications/factbook/geos/nz.html
www.defence.govt.nz
www.navy.mil.nz
www.army.mil.nz
www.airforce.mil.nz
www.treasury.govt.nz

Population

Population clock

US Bureau of the Census: www.census.gov/main/www/pop-clock.html

Immigration

www.stats.govt.nz
www.immigration.govt.nz

Language

www.aotearoalive.com
www.kohanga.ac.nz
www.maori.org.nz
www.stats.govt.nz

Social framework

The Social Report 2001, Ministry of Social Development: www.msd.govt.nz
Youth Development Strategy Aotearoa (February 2002) Ministry of Youth Affairs: www.youthaffairs.govt.nz
www.treasury.govt.nz
'Client Quarterly Profile' June 2001: www.winz.govt.nz

Health

Health data

The Social Report 2001, Ministry of Social Development: www.msd.govt.nz

An indication of New Zealanders' Health, 2002. Ministry of Health: www.moh.govt.nz/phi

An Overview of the Health and Disability Sector in New Zealand (Ministry of Health, November 2001), on: www.moh.govt.nz

www.treasury.govt.nz

Accidents

www.acc.co.nz

www.osh.dol.govt.nz

www.ltsa.govt.nz

www.transport.govt.nz

www.watersafety.org.nz

Fire statistics

The New Zealand Fire Service: www.fire.org.nz

Youth suicide

New Zealand Health Information Service: www.nzhis.govt.nz/stats/youthsuicide.html

An indication of New Zealanders' Health, 2002. Ministry of Health: www.moh.govt.nz/phi

Youth suicide prevention strategies, see: www.youthaffairs.govt.nz

Drug abuse

National Drug Policy unit: www.ndp.govt.nz

New Zealand Health Information Service:

www.nzhis.govt.nz/publications/drugs.html

The Alcohol Advisory Council: www.alcohol.org.nz

Sexual health

Sexual and Reproductive Health Strategy, on: www.moh.govt.nz

Education

www.mosp.govt.nz

Education agencies

'The Social Report 2001', on: www.msd.govt.nz

www.minedu.govt.nz

www.treasury.govt.nz

National qualifications

NCEA: www.nzqa.govt.nz/ncea

Corrections system

www.corrections.govt.nz

www.justice.govt.nz

www.police.govt.nz

www.prisonstudies.org

www.courts.govt.nz

www.decisionmaker.co.nz/guide/parliament

Creation and recreation

www.nzmuseums.co.nz

The Ministry for Culture and Heritage: www.mch.govt.nz

www.creativenz.govt.nz

http://url.co.nz/arts/nzarts.html

http://tepuna.natlib.govt.nz/web_directory/NZ/serials.htm

www.piperpat.co.nz/nz/culture/general.html

Top ten songs

Australasian Performing Rights Association: www.apra.co.nz

www.nzmusic.org.nz

www.rianz.org.nz/index.cfm

Reading and writing

www.freedomhouse.org.

Book awards

www.vuw.ac.nz/nzbookcouncil/awards/montana.htm

Children's Literature Foundation of NZ: www.clfnz.org.nz

children's literature awards: http://lib.cce.ac.nz/nzcba/intro.html

Libraries

www.localgovt.co.nz

www.natlib.govt.nz/flash.html

Film and video

http://tepuna.natlib.govt.nz/web_directory/NZ/film.htm

www.filmsite.org

The New Zealand Film Archive: www.nzfa.org.nz

The New Zealand Film Commission: www.nzfilm.co.nz

'Scoping the Lasting Effects of *The Lord of the Rings.* Report to The New Zealand Film Commission', NZ Institute of Economic Research (Inc.), April 2002, on: www.nzfilm.co.nz

Television

Natural History New Zealand Limited: www.naturalhistory.co.nz

'Local New Zealand television content 2001', on: www.nzonair.govt.nz

Radio

www.radionz.co.nz

Sport and leisure

www.piperpat.co.nz/nz/sport/

www.athletics.org.nz

www.sportnz.co.nz

www.olympic.org.nz

www.paralympicsnz.org.nz

www.nzrugby.co.nz

www.netballnz.co.nz/

www.halberg.co.nz/SportsChampionoftheCentury.htm

The New Zealand Sports Hall of Fame: www.nzhalloffame.co.nz

Statistics New Zealand, *Time Use Survey 1999*, on: www.stats.govt.nz

An indication of New Zealanders' Health, 2002. Ministry of Health: www.moh.govt.nz/phi

Gaming and betting

Department of Internal Affairs: www.dia.govt.nz

Section 3: Resources and economy

Resources

www.landcare.cri.nz

www.maf.govt.nz (Ministry of Agriculture & Forestry for water management guidelines)

www.moh.govt.nz (Ministry of Health on drinking water quality)

www.morst.govt.nz (Ministry of Research, Science and Technology)

Crown Minerals. *Explore New Zealand Minerals*, on: www.med.govt.nz/crown_minerals

New Zealand Energy Data File January 2002, on: www.med.govt.nz/ers/en_stats.html

Chronology of New Zealand Electricity Reform, on: www.med.govt.nz/ers/electric/chronology/index.html

Income and work/spending

www.stats.govt.nz

'The Social Report 2001', on: www.msd.govt.nz

Department of Labour: www.dol.govt.nz

Infrastructure

Communications

Ministry of Economic Development: www.med.govt.nz

The Telecommunications Users Association of New Zealand: www.tuanz.org.nz

Information Technology Association of New Zealand: www.itanz.org.nz

Postal services
www.nzpost.co.nz
www.kiwibank.co.nz

Transport
www.tranzrail.co.nz
www.airnz.co.nz
www.transit.govt.nz
www.transport.govt.nz
www.stats.govt.nz

Customs
www.customs.govt.nz

Money facts
New Zealand Bankers' Association: www.nzba.org.nz

Environment
The State of New Zealand's Environment 1997, on: www.mfe.govt.nz/about/publications/ser/ser.htm

Creating our future: sustainable development for New Zealand, 2002. Commissioner for the Environment, on: www.pce.govt.nz

New Zealand Energy Data File January 2002, on: www.med.govt.nz/ers/en_stats.html

Redefining Progress, on: www.rprogress.org/programs/sustainability/ef

Primary production

Agriculture, horticulture and forestry
www.maf.govt.nz

Pastoral agriculture
www.nzmeat.co.nz
www.woolgroup.co.nz
www.pianz.org.nz
www.fonterra.com

Crops and horticulture
www.zespri.com
www.nzwine.com
www.maf.govt.nz
Fishing/aquaculture
Ministry of Fisheries: www.fish.govt.nz
New Zealand Seafood Industry Council: www.seafood.co.nz

Tourism
www.fishnhunt.co.nz
www.stats.govt.nz
www.purenz.com
Travel Agents Association of New Zealand: www.taanz.org.nz

Science and technology
www.stats.govt.nz
Kiwi ingenuity
www.britten.co.nz
www.dnzb.govt.nz
www.no8wire.co.nz
www.nzedge.com

Overseas merchandise trade/National finance
www.stats.govt.nz

Information for visitors
www.purenz.com

Index

abortions 146
Accident Compensation Corporation (ACC) 135
accidents 139; traffic 136; water 138
accommodation, tourist 242
Act 82
Acts of Parliament 82
agriculture 226, 228, 229
Ahuriri Wetlands 38
aid: bilateral 100; development 99; multilateral 100; NZ Agency for International Development 100; NZ's Official Development Assistance 100
AIDS 146
Air Force, Royal NZ 102
airports 220
alcohol 134, 141
All Blacks 65
Alliance 82
America's Cup 191
amphibians 49
animals, introduced and native 31
Anniversary Days 171
Antarctic Treaty 101
Antarctica 101
anthems, national 96
Anzac Day 104
ANZUS Treaty 66, 102
Aoraki/Mt Cook 16
Aotearoa Traditional Maori Performing Arts Festival 174
apples 234
aquaculture 239
Arapawa Island 15
Army, NZ 102; peace-keeping commitments 103
arrivals, international 112, 221; canoes 70; overseas visitors 241
art galleries 174
arts and culture 172
arts, performing, organisations 175
Asia Pacific Economic Cooperation (APEC) 98
Asian Development Bank 98
Associated Queen's Service Medal 93
Association of South East Asian Nations (ASEAN) 99
Auckland Zoo 50
authorities, special 90, 91
aviation, civil 220

balance of payments 250
Banks Peninsula 58
bats: 42; NZ lesser short-tailed 42; NZ long-tailed bat 42
Beehive 95
betting, race 194
biosecurity 253
birds 36; extremes 37; endangered 40, extinctions 39, 40; flightless 36; lice 56; rare 38
births 109, 120; rate 110
Black Stilt Viewing Hide 38
Bolger, Jim 67
books, awards, 176; children's 177
Bravery Awards 93, 94
bridges 219

broadcasting 65
business hours 252
butterflies 56

Cabinet 85
calderas 21
Campbell Island 14
Campion, Jane 179
cannabis 143
canoes, arrival 70
cargo 221
Carter Observatory 245
casinos 192, 194
cats 48; feral 47
caves 18; deepest 18; longest 18
Cawthron Institute 245
Census 105
central government 80; finance 251
chamois 47
Chatham Island 14
Chatham Islands/Rekohu 74; Time 7
Child Support Act 1992 120
childbearing 119
chlamydia 145
cigarette smoking 131
cities 109
citizen's initiated referenda (CIR) 88
Clark, Helen 67
climate, extremes 24; in four main cities 24
Closer Economic Relations (CER) 67
coal 201
coat of arms, NZ 95
Colleges of Education 159
Commonwealth 98
Commonwealth Games 189; Auckland 190
communications 213
community boards 91
computer, use 213
conservation issues 60
Conservation, Department of (DOC) 58, 223
constellations 10
Constitution 77
Consumers Price Index (CPI) 211
Cook Islands 66, 101
Cook Strait 23
Cook, James 63, 70
Corrections, Department of 167
corrections system 166
Correspondence School 155
Corruption Perceptions Index 89
councils, regional 90
courts 87, 163; Court of Appeal 87, 163; District Court 87, 163; Family Court 87; High Court 87, 163; specialist 163
credit cards 252
criminal, convictions 165, 169; justice 165; offences 169
crime, recorded 165
Crowe, Russell 179
Crown entities 85
Crown Law Office 164
Crown Research Institutes (CRIs) 245
Culture and Heritage, Ministry of 95
Curio Bay 11
currency 252; decimal 66; foreign 252

Curriculum Framework, The New Zealand 156
Customs, New Zealand 222

dairy: exports 231; farms 230; industry 230; products 229
Daylight Time, New Zealand 7
De Surville, Jean 70
deaths 109; in volcanic areas 22
debt 207
Declaration of Independence 63
deer: fallow 47; red 48
defence 102; expenditure 103, 104; personnel 104
Defence Force, NZ 102
dental health 145
departments, government 85
departures, international 112, 221
Development, NZ Agency for International 100
Development Assistance, NZ's Official 100
diabetes 135
diet 134
diplomatic, posts 98; representatives 98
disasters 147
Disputes Tribunals 87
District Health Boards (DHBs) 132
divorce 117, 118; rate 118
dog (kuri) 42
dolphins: 44; Hector's 45
Domestic Purposes Benefit 128
Domestic Violence Act 1995 120
Dominion 65
drink driving 136, 142
driver licences 217
drugs, illicit 144
drownings 139
duck: grey 42; mallard 42
D'Urville Island 15

earthquakes 65; fatalities 20; Wairarapa 20; Wellington fault line 21
ecological footprint 225
education 149; agencies 151; compulsory 154; early childhood 154; home-schooling 155; qualifications 156, 210; spending 152, 153; tertiary 150, 158
Education Act 1877 64
Education, Ministry of 149
Edward VII 77
Edward VIII 77
eels 54, 55
El Niño 26
elections 65
Electoral Act 1993 81
Electoral Districts 81
electorates 81
electricity 253; generation 200
Elizabeth II 77
emergency services 253
employment 205, 207; % by industry type 243; legislation 209; in primary production 228; unemployment 207
Employment Contracts Act 1991 67, 209
Employment Relations Act 2000 209
endangered species: fish 54; marine mammals 45; reptiles 52

endemic species 28
energy: consumer 197, 198; geothermal 198; primary sources 196; renewable 202; resources 196; supplies 197, 199; transformation 197
English 123; speakers 123
Environment Court 87
Environment, Ministry for the 223
Environment, Parliamentary Commissioner for the 223
environmental, issues 223
environmental organisations 99
ethnic groups 114
ethnicity 113
Exclusive Economic Zone 55, 67
executions 170
Executive 80, 82
Executive Council 85
expenditure, government 86
exports 220; by commodity 249; by country 248; of forestry products 236

Family Proceedings Act 1980 120
family size 110
farms by type 230
ferret, feral 47
ferries, inter-island 220
fertility rate 110
Festival, Aotearoa Traditional Maori Performing Arts 174
Festival, NZ 175
festival, Pasifika 174
film 178
Film Commission, NZ 180
financial institutions 222
Fiordland National Park 58
Fire Service, NZ 139
fire statistics 140
First World War 65
fish 53; freshwater 53; galaxids 54; marine 55; native 54
Fisheries, Ministry of 238
fishing industry 237; markets 238; major export species 238
fitness 182
Five Power Defence Arrangements 102
flag, NZ 95
flowers, cut 235
Fonterra Co-operative Group Ltd 231
Foreign Affairs and Trade, Ministry of 98
Forest and Bird Protection Society of NZ, Royal 37, 39
forestry 226, 228, 235
forests 33; beech 34; coastal 34; conifer-hardwoods 33; mangrove 34; montane 34; secondary 34; swamp 34
Foveaux Strait 23
frogs 49, 52, 53; Archey's 52; Hamilton's 52; Hochstetter's 52; Maud Island 52
fruit 235

Gallantry Awards 93
Gallipoli 65
gambling 194
gaming, expenditure 193; machines 192, 193, 194
gas 201; Maui field 200
geckos 50
General Assembly 64; Library 95

geographical extremes 19
George V 77
George VI 77
glaciers 16; largest 16
'God Defend New Zealand' 96
'God Save the Queen' 97
godwit 37
gold 203
goldrushes 64, 68
Gondwana 11, 28
Goods and Services Tax (GST) 67, 253
government departments 85
government ministries 95, 129, 131, 149, 223, 238
government, local 90, 91
Governor-General 77, 78
Governors 78
gratuities 253
Great Barrier Island 15
Great Walks of NZ 60
Green 82
greenhouse gas emissions 224
greenstone 204
Guardianship Act 1968 120

haka 187
hare, brown 46
Hauraki Gulf 45
health: issues 134; spending 133; system 131
Health, Ministry of 131
hebes 35
hedgehog 46
helmets 217
Hillary, Edmund 66
Historic Places Trust, NZ, Pouhere Taonga 76
historic sites 76
HIV 146
Hobson, William 63
holidays 209; Anniversary Days 171; statutory 171
home ownership 223
Hone Heke 64
honey 235
Hongi Hika 63
honours system 91
horse, feral 47
horse breeding 192
horticulture 226, 228, 233; crops 233; exports 233; production 233
hospitalisation 135
household: composition 117; spending 211
Household Savings Survey 206
housing 223
Howard, Mabel 88
huhu 56
huia 40
humidity 24
hydroelectric generation 195

immigrants, birthplace 114
immigration 68
imports 220; by commodity 249; by country 248
Inch Clutha 15
income, personal 206, 207; sources 205; summary 205
income, government 86
industry groups 243
infant mortality 130
influenza epidemic 65
information technology 247

insects 32; introduced and native 31
Internal Affairs, Department of 193
International Labour Organisation (ILO) 98
Internet 214
inventions 246
invertebrates 56
iron 203
island territories 14
islands: largest offshore 15; main and outlying islands 14
iwi (Maori tribes) 70, 73

Jim Anderton's Progressive Coalition 82
judiciary 80, 87
jury service 164
Justice, Department of 167

kahikatea 35
Kaikoura 45
kakapo 37
katipo spider 28, 57
kauri 35
King Movement 76
Kingitanga 76
kiore/Polynesian rat 42, 46
kiwi 36, 41
Kiwibank 216
kiwifruit 233
knot, great 37
Kohanga Reo, Te 124
kokako, South Island 41
Korean War 66
Kotahitanga Maori Parliament 76
kunekune 47
Kura Kaupapa Maori 155
kuri/Maori dog 42, 47, 48

La Niña 26
Labour 65, 82
Labour Day 172
labour force: changes 208; participation 208; total 207
lakes, largest 17
lamprey 54
land use 226
Land Wars 64
languages 123; official 123
law: common 163; NZ 163
Law Commission, The 163
legal aid 164
legal system 163
Legislation Chamber 95
Legislature 80
leisure activities, outdoor 191; physical 134; popular 240
libraries 178
Library, National 176, 178
Lieutenant-Governors 78
life expectancy 111, 130
literacy 149
Little Barrier Island 15
livestock 229
living, standard of 125, 127
lizards 50
local government 90; community boards 91
Lord of the Rings 178, 179, 180
Lotteries Commission 194

magazines 176
Malaghan Institute of Medical Research 245

Malaspina, Don Alessandro 70
mammals 32, 42, 46; introduced 31, 46; marine 43; native 31, 42
Manawatu Estuary 38
manufacturing 243
Manufacturing, Quarterly Economic Survey of 244
Maori 123; arts 173; electoral roll 82; electorate seats 82; Kings 76; proverbs 124; Queens 76; speakers 124
Margaret Mahy Award 177
marine fish 55
marine mammals 43; sanctuaries 58
marine parks and reserves 58
Marine Reserve, Kermadec Islands 58
marriages 117, 118; de facto 117, 118
marsupials 46
Matakana Island 15
Matrimonial Property Act 1976 120
Maui 45
McCombs, Elizabeth 88
meat and meat products 229, 231; consumption 232
Members of Parliament (MPs) 80; electorate 80; list 80
metric system 66
migration 111, 112; permanent and long-term 221
Milford Sound 45
mineral resources 202; non-metallic 203
ministries, government 95, 129, 131, 149, 223, 238
Miranda 38
Mixed Member Proportional (MMP): election 67; system 80
moa, giant 37
money 252
Montana NZ Book Awards 176
moose 48
Moriori 74
mortality, causes 147
mosquitoes 57
moth, puriri (ghost) 56
Motor Vehicle Disputes Tribunal 87
motor vehicles 117
mountains, highest 15; North Island 16
mouse, house 46
Mt Bruce National Wildlife Centre 38, 50
Mt Cook/Aoraki 16
Mt Tarawera 64
mudfish 54
Museum of NZ Te Papa Tongarewa 174
museums 174
Musket Wars 63
Mutual Assistance Programme 102

National 65, 82
national accounts aggregates 250
National Airways Corporation 66
National Alcohol Survey 141
national anthems 96
National Certificate of Educational Achievement, The (NCEA) 156
National Drugs Survey 144

National Gambling Prevalence Survey 193
National Library 176, 178
national parks 58, 60
National Poison Centre 145
National Prevalence Survey 194
National Qualifications Framework 157
Native Land Court 64
Natural History NZ Ltd 182
Naval Forces, Royal NZ 102
Neill, Sam 178
nettle, native 35
NZ Bill of Rights Act 1990 82
New Zealand First 82
NZ Post Limited 216
newspapers 176
Ngarimu, Moananui-a-kiwi 94

Occupational Health and Safety 139
offences 169
oil 200; reserves 200
Old Age Pensions Act 1898 65
Olympics 188
Once Were Warriors 178, 179
ongaonga 35
Opo 45
Order of Chivalry 93
Order of Merit, NZ 91, 93
Order of New Zealand 91, 92
Organisation for Economic Cooperation and Development (OECD) 98; comparisons 116, 149
Orion 10
Oscar winners 179
ozone hole 27

Pacific arts 174
Pacific Island Forum 99
Pacific Island peoples 69
parental leave, paid 210
Paquin, Anna 179
Paralympics 189
parks: conservation (forest) 58; national 58, 60
Parliament 80; buildings 95
Pasifika festival 174
Passchendaele, Battle of 65
payment methods 222
peace-keeping commitments 103
pears 234
Pearse, Richard 65
Pelorus Jack 45
penal institutions 166
peripatus 57
pests 32
pigmeat 232
pipfruit industry 234
Pitt Island 14
plants 32; introduced and native 31; divaricate 35; noxious 32
Pointers 10
Poison Centre, National 145
Police, NZ 168; operations 170
Polynesian settlement 63
polytechnics 158
Pompallier, Bishop 63
Poolburn 11
population 106; ageing 109; change 109, 115; de facto 107; usually resident 107
porpoises 44, 45
ports 219, 220
possum 233

postal services 216
Potatau Te Wherowhero 76
Potatau Te Wherowhero Mahuta 76
Potatau Te Wherowhero Te Rata 76
poultry 232
Premiers 83
primary producers 227
primary production 226; value 227
Prime Ministers 83
prison population 165
prisons programme, regional 167
Privy Council 87; Judicial Committee of 163
Property (Relationships) Act 1976 120
provinces 91
Public Service, NZ 85
punishment, capital 170

qualifications 210; national 156; tertiary 160
Quality of Life Project 108
Quarantine Services 222
Queen's Service Order 91, 93
Quota Management System 238

rabbit 46
radio, 182
rail 219
Rainbow Warrior 67
rainfall 23, 24
Rangitoto Island 15
Raoul Island 14
rat: Norway 47; Polynesian (kiore) 42; ship 47
Ratana, Tahupotiki Wiremu 76
Reefton 65
referendum issues, results 88, 89
religions 121, 122
Representation Commission 81
reptiles 49
Reserve Bank of NZ 222, 223
reserves 58
Resolution Island 15
Resource Management Act 1991 224
retail trade sales 211
revenue, government 86
Ringatu 76
rivers, longest 17
road toll 137, 169
road transport 217
roads 217
Ross Dependency 14, 101
Royal Albatross Centre 38
Royal Forest and Bird Protection Society of NZ 37, 39
Royal Honours System, NZ 91
Royal Society of NZ 245
Rutherford, Ernest 65, 246

salmon 54
salt 204
sandfly 56
savings 206
schools: boarding 155; curriculum 156; independent (private) 155; intermediate 154; primary 154; secondary 154; state 155; terms 153; types 155
Scorpius 10
sea lions 43; Hooker's 43
seabirds 28
Sealord Products Ltd 238

seals: fur (eared seals) 43; true 43
seatbelt use 138
Second World War 66
Secretary Island 15
sentencing, community-based 166
sexual health 145
sexually transmitted infection (STI) rates 145
sheep farms 230
sheepmeat 232
Shipley, Jenny 67
shipping 219
silver 203
skinks 50, 51
smoking 134, 142
snails 57
snow 25; sports 26
Social Development, Ministry for 149
Social Security Act 1938 66, 125
Social Welfare expenditure 128
social welfare legislation 125
soil 195; Soil Classification 195
Somes Island 50
songs 175
South African War 65
Southern Alps 15, 25
Southern Cross 10
Southern Temperate Zone 23
Southland Museum 50
Sovereigns of NZ 77
speed limits 218
spiders 57
sports 182, 185; club 184; injuries 187; most popular 186, 187
sportspeople 183
springs, hot water 22
state sector 85
State-owned Enterprises (SOEs) 85
Stewart Island 14, 38
stick insect 56
stoat 47, 48
Student Allowance 128
student loan scheme 128, 161
students 152; international 157
Sub-Antarctic Islands Reserve, NZ 60
Sugar Loaf Islands 58; Marine Reserve 45
sunshine 24
Superannuation, NZ 66, 128

tahr, Himalayan 48
taiko, Chatham Island 37
takahe 38
Tasman, Abel 63, 70
Taupo Volcanic Zone 21
Tawhiao (Potatau II) 76
taxes 253
Te Atairangikahu 76
Te Kohanga Reo 124
Te Kooti, Arikirangi Te Turuki 64, 76
Te Puna Matauranga 178
Te Rauparaha 63, 187
Te Wahipounamu 60
Te Wherowhero, Tawhiao Potatau 76
Te Wherowhero family 76
teacher training 162
Telecom NZ Ltd 213
telecommunications 213; mobile phones 213
television 180
temperature 23, 24
tern, fairy 37

territorial authorities 90
territorial councils 90
territories, NZ 101
taxa, threatened 29
tipping 253
timber, sawn 237
Time, NZ Standard 7
Tiritiri Matangi Island 37, 50
Titokowaru, Riwha 64
Tokelaus 14, 101
Tongariro National Park 60
Totaliser Agency Board (TAB) 192
tourism 240, 241
tourist accommodation 242
traffic accidents 136
Transit NZ 217
transport 216
Tranz Rail 219
travel 221
Treaty of Friendship 69
Treaty of Waitangi 64, 74, 77; settlements 75
Treaty Settlements, Office of 75
trees (see forests, and under individual species)
tribunals 87, 163
trout 54
tuatara 49

ultraviolet (UV) levels, 27
unemployment 207
Unemployment Benefit 128
United Future 82
United Nations 99, 102
universities 159
University of Otago 64
Upham, Charles 94
urbanisation comparisons 108

vegetables 235; exports 235
vehicles: fuel use 200; numbers 218; use 217
venison 232
viaducts 219
Victoria (Queen) 77
Victoria Cross 94
video 178
Vietnam 66
volcanoes 21, 22; calderas 21
von Tunzelmann, Alexander 101
voting 64

wage, minimum 210
Waiheke Island 15
Wairarapa earthquake 20
Waitangi Tribunal 66, 75, 87
wananga 159
war casualties 103
'War in the North' 64
War: First World 65; Second World 66; South African 65
water 195, 253; consumption 195; quality 195
water accidents 138
Water Safety NZ 138
weasel 47, 48
Wellington fault line 21
weta 57
whales 29, 44; baleen 44; pilot 44
White Heron colony, Okarito 38
wine 234
women in power 88
wool 229, 232
working hours 209
World Bank 99

world heritage sites 60
World Trade Organisation (WTO) 99
wren, bush 37
wren, Stephen's Island 40
wrybill, NZ 39
Yates, Elizabeth 88
Yellow-eyed Penguin Conservation Reserve 38
Youth Affairs, Ministry of 129
Youth Court 87
youth suicide 130, 140